Wish you were here ...

Jersey holidays in picture postcards

John Le Dain

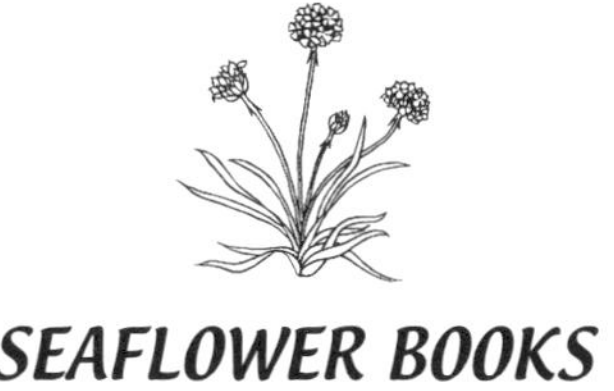

SEAFLOWER BOOKS

Published in 2014 by
SEAFLOWER BOOKS
11 Regents Place
Bradford on Avon
Wiltshire BA15 1JS

A longer and larger format edition of this book, under a similar title, was published by Seaflower in 2002 and has been out of print for some years prior to publication of this briefer, smaller format version

www.ex-librisbooks.co.uk

Printed by CPI Anthony Rowe
Chippenham
Wiltshire

ISBN 978-1-906641-63-4

Acknowledgements

To David Le Maistre who gave of his time and generously allowed me to plug a few gaps by allowing me to take copies of five postcards from his personal collection. They are on pages 14, 31, 50, 99 and 124.
To the late Brian Ahier for his useful comments.
To all those correspondents whose holiday jottings are quoted in these pages.

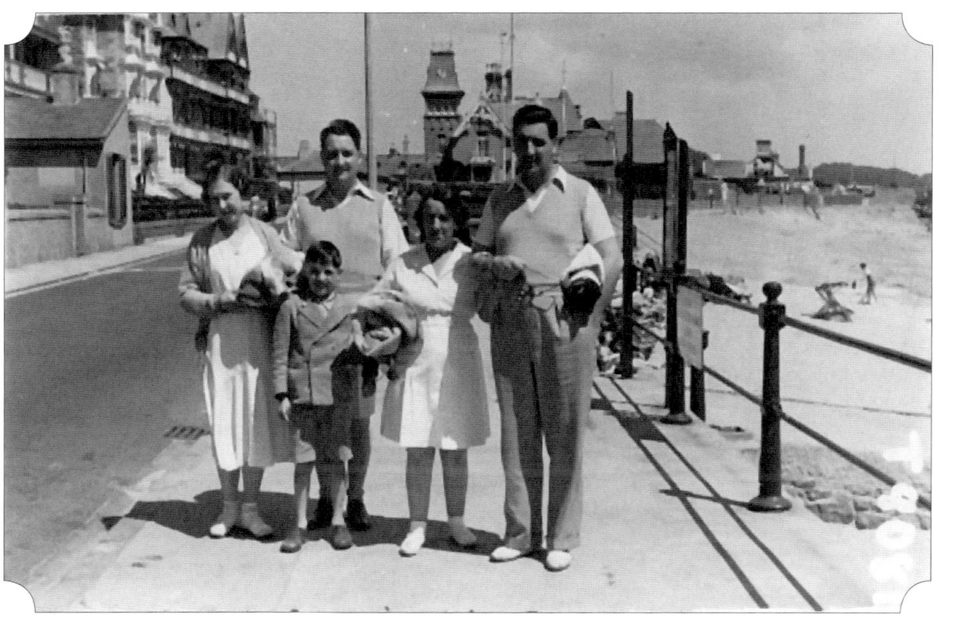

Photograph taken by itinerant photographer and printed by 'HAPPY SNAPS' of Broad Street. The owner noted the date 1936 and the names, from left to right: 'Self, Bert, Dick, Edie, Frank. The picture shows the group with their towels preparing to take a dip from the beach at Havre des Pas, or perhaps at the Bathing Pool which had been in existence since 1895.

Contents ~

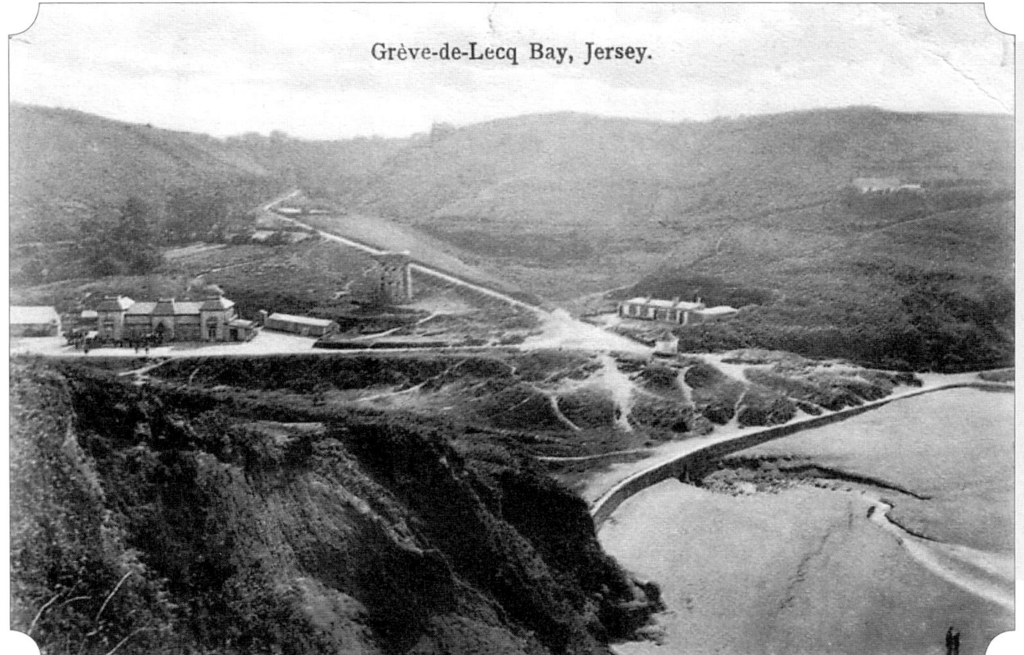

'Have had another topping day. We walked over to Plémont this morning and then on to Grève de Lecq whence we turned our steps homeward. Reckon we must have covered something like 20 miles & as there is a whist drive and dance on tonight expect to feel tired. We wandered into town last night and purchased a small bottle of D.O.M. so indulge in a nightcap when we get upstairs. I find it helps H.S. from snoring.'

L.C.

This postcard was sent to E.H. Pope Esq., Bromley, Kent and postmarked June 25th, 1913, and displays a view of a much less developed Grève de Lecq – far fewer buildings and no car parks.

Introduction

The idea for the first edition of this book, published in 2002, was prompted when I wandered into an Antiques Fair in Cirencester. One of the stallholders was a picture postcard dealer who stood watch over trays full of old postcards, including a large section devoted to places, especially the British Isles, organised under county headings. At the end of the A-Z sequence was Yorkshire, followed by the Channel Islands, detached here as they are on the map. I found a couple of interesting Jersey items – one an early view of Grève de Lecq (see opposite), the other a composite view (see overleaf), When I turned them over I found myself riveted by the messages. Each postcard offers a double-faceted glimpse of Jersey at the time of its sending – a view of the island and evidence of the sender's holiday experience.

~

Postcard collecting as a hobby rapidly grew in popularity. People sent postcards to their friends not simply to convey a message but in order to boost that friend's postcard collection and they would expect a postcard in return. People accumulated collections and swapped duplicates. Today, postcards of the Edwardian era are more commonplace than those of the interwar period – not necessarily because more were sent, which is unlikely, but because more were collected for posterity. More holidaymakers had cameras after the First World War so they accumulated photograph albums as holiday keepsakes rather than the more impersonal postcard collections.

Probably the majority of old Jersey postcards in circulation today were sent by holidaymakers to family and friends at home or, perhaps more often, simply purchased as holiday souvenirs. In the latter case the cards will be without a written message, always a disappointment. A significant minority of Jersey postcards were sent and received locally, within the island. Postcards became a means of communication for locals – some of the messages are wonderfully intriguing even when one feels one is snooping into the lives of strangers, but irresistable.

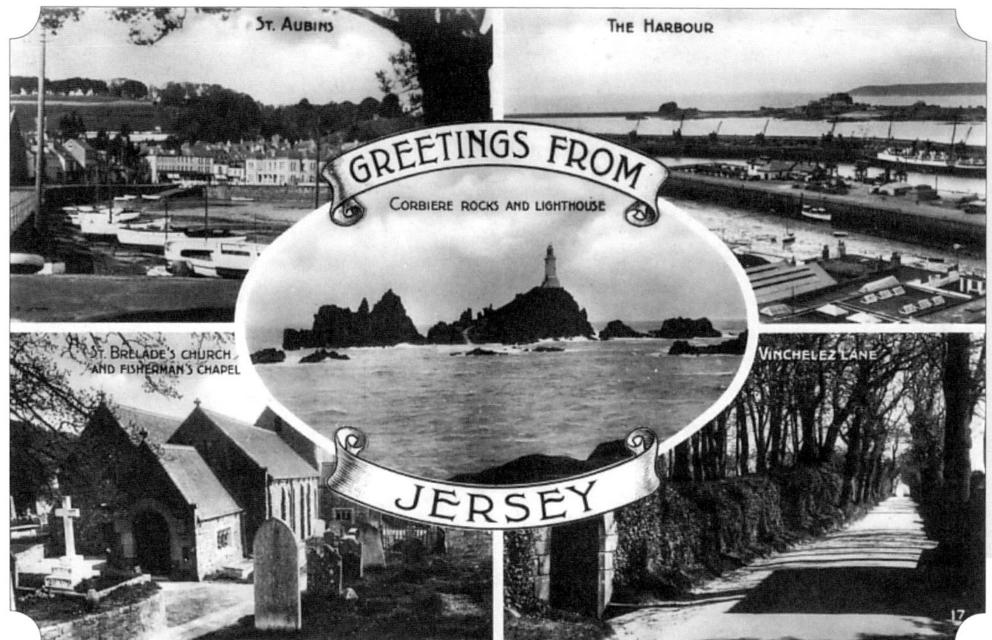

'Willrose
43, Kensington Place

A greeting from an old pal to remind you of the good old days!!! Have been attempting to visit you since Xmas to thank you for flowers. Shall manage it one day. It is glorious here (once you arrive). Plenty of sunshine and shops full of food. Can recommend this place if you want a carefree holiday. Love to George, the Capt. & Self.

Grace'

Grace's card is postmarked 2nd July, 1946, the first holiday season after the Liberation. She had apparently visited Jersey before the war, in 'the good old days', and seems extremely happy to be back. The comment that 'shops full of food' is made in contrast to the experience of strict rationing in mainland Britain at this time.

In the days of a super-efficient postal service, with several collections and deliveries daily, people used postcards to transmit brief written messages, just as we use the telephone, text and e-mail today. Postcard writing is, perhaps, not quite as radical a literary form as texting, but normal rules of grammar, and certainly of punctuation, usually do not apply. In the absence of commas and stops sentences tend to run together so that postcard correspondents often seem to be in a hurry. Which of course they were, dutifully writing to all and sundry at home when what they would perhaps rather have been doing was enjoying their holiday.

~

However, the focus of this little book is on the postcards which tourists sent home, and what the views and the messages reveal about the story of Jersey as a holiday destination. The development of tourism is as much an aspect of our social history as education or women's rights or anything else. But tourism is predominantly a happy subject, a point that is repeatedly emphasised in the messages people write on postcards.

~

Tourism in Jersey first developed during the Napoleonic Wars, at the beginning of the nineteenth century, when continental travel became difficult for the British. The first guide book for tourists – Stead's *A Picture of Jersey, or Stranger's Companion through that Island*, was published in 1809, and this was followed by many more. Such guide books sought to direct the visitor around the island, and provide a commentary on places seen and on history and culture. Such books began appearing before the age of photography and were illustrated, if at all, with engravings – often rather inaccurate representations of local scenes. The first Jersey postcards appeared in 1897 and the number of cards and range of subjects grew rapidly thereafter.

As their target audience, the postcard manufacturers probably had in mind the holidaymakers whose numbers increased steadily towards the end of the nineteenth century and the early years of the twentieth. But one wonders how many tourists would choose a postcard of the Female Orphans' Home, or Dr Barnardo's Home for Little Boys at Gorey, such institutions not constituting priority holiday destinations. Others were produced to promote local businesses: hotels, cafes, shops. And yet others were made from pictures taken by itinerant photographers who often specialised in snapping groups – most often at the outset of a charabanc outing, or in front of a hotel. Copies of these pictures would then be available next day for persons in the group to purchase.

The advent of the postcard coincided with the growing popularity of tourism in Jersey. Indeed, tourism rivalled agriculture as the island's biggest employer and revenue earner until the rise of the finance industry in the 1970s. Today the outlook for tourism is not encouraging: hotels and guest houses continue to close, beach cafés, tourist attractions and car hire firms also. It seems a shame ... or am I just being nostalgic, having personally enjoyed holidays in Jersey every year since I can remember – since 1945, in fact. A place which has given so much pleasure to so many people for so many years must be special. Well, of course, Jersey is special, with its golden beaches, rocky headlands, wooded valleys and delicious countryside. And all those thousands of holidays and the generations of visitors who have enjoyed them have surely lent Jersey a kind of aura, or is it simply that it's such a beautiful island?

~

All the images in this book are reproduced in black and white because the originals were printed in black ink, or sepia ink, on white card. Colour postcards are as old as monochrome, though far less commonplace. They were often black and white images which had been tinted with occasionally bizarre results. Until the 1930s, postcards were printed by a process known as photogravure. The advent of photographic cards was a matter of pride and the legend 'This is a Real Photograph' was proclaimed on the message side. These were indeed real photographs and did not go through the screening process which for many years now has been a preliminary to offset litho printing.

Early postcards vary hugely in quality – some present clear and well-lit images whilst others are rather poor: woolly grey images lacking much detail. Even with modern computer scanning and image enhancement capability it is difficult to improve much on such inferior images.

Monochrome postcards were replaced by colour around 1970 and probably best illustrate the heyday of tourism in Jersey and therefore the current book. I hope you enjoy it.

John Le Dain, 2014

~ Arrival ~

Steam ships began replacing sail around the beginning of the nineteenth century. The greater frequency and improved punctuality of sea connections between Jersey and the mainland enabled a steady increase in the number of visitors and to the development of tourism as a local industry

There were sailings from a variety of ports on England's south coast; there was even a direct sailing from London which took 26 hours. However, the two main routes were the Great Western Railway (GWR) from Weymouth and the London and South Western Railway (GWR) – later the Southern Railway (SR) – from Southampton. However, by the 1920s these two companies ran their services in conjunction and sponsored joint advertising of their 'Daily Service between England & Jersey by Large Twin-Screw and Turbine Steamers'.

A succession of boats served these two companies which, after rail nationalisation in 1948, became British Railways, then Sealink. Whether sailing from Weymouth or Southampton, the journey was a long one. Excitement at the prospect of the voyage was often tempered by anticipation of a rough crossing and seasickness. Many postcards home start with a report on the crossing and correspondents often remark, 'Dreadful crossing, but it was worth it!'

Air services began in 1933, when small biplanes from England landed on the beach at West Park prior to the opening of Jersey Airport in 1937. The Occupation stopped tourism in its tracks but the German occupiers at least improved the airport by lengthening its runways.

After 1945 air services grew steadily but the cheaper boat services held their own and began to fight back with the introduction of high-speed hydrofoils in the 1970s and, subsequently, of spacious, car-carrying catamarans.

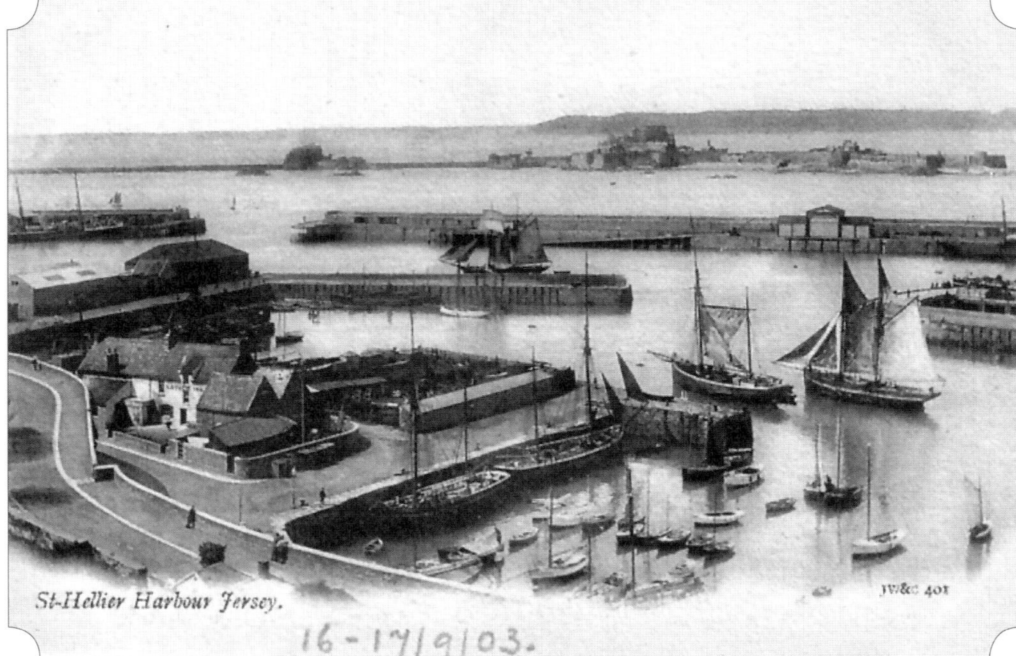

'Dear Nan,
Just to let you know we have recovered from a very rough crossing here, it was terrible. The sun is shining today and we hope to bathe later.'
(Message sent 1956)

~

'Had a rough crossing but managed to sleep and keep fit until after Guernsey – then, oh dear, I had it! Shall return by air on Tuesday'
(Message sent 1940?)

View of St Helier Harbour taken from Pier Road. The person who sent this card noted the date 16th/17th September, 1903, and we can see that we are very much still in the age of sail. La Folie Inn can be seen middle left.

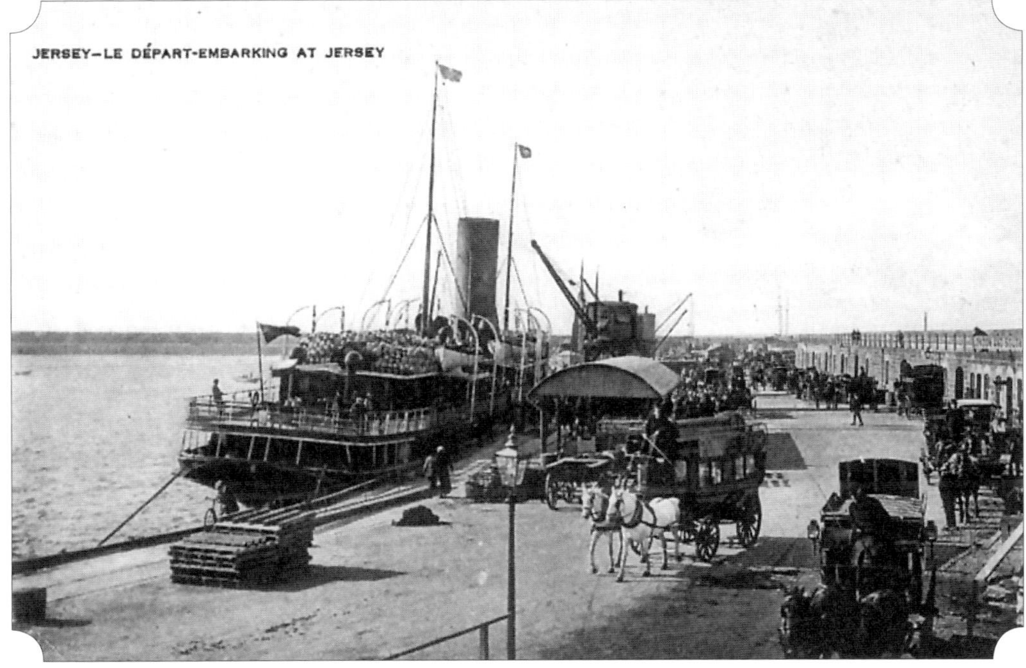

'We arrived at Jersey safely last night at 9.30, there was no morning boat. We were caught in a fearful thunderstorm last Saturday and this morning it is showery but fearfully hot.
Love from Daisy'

Unidentified ship, possibly SS *Lydia*, unloading passengers at the Abert Pier. Hotels often provided their own transport to collect guests arriving at the harbour. The coach being pulled by the two white horses, middle foreground, is from the Pomme D'Or

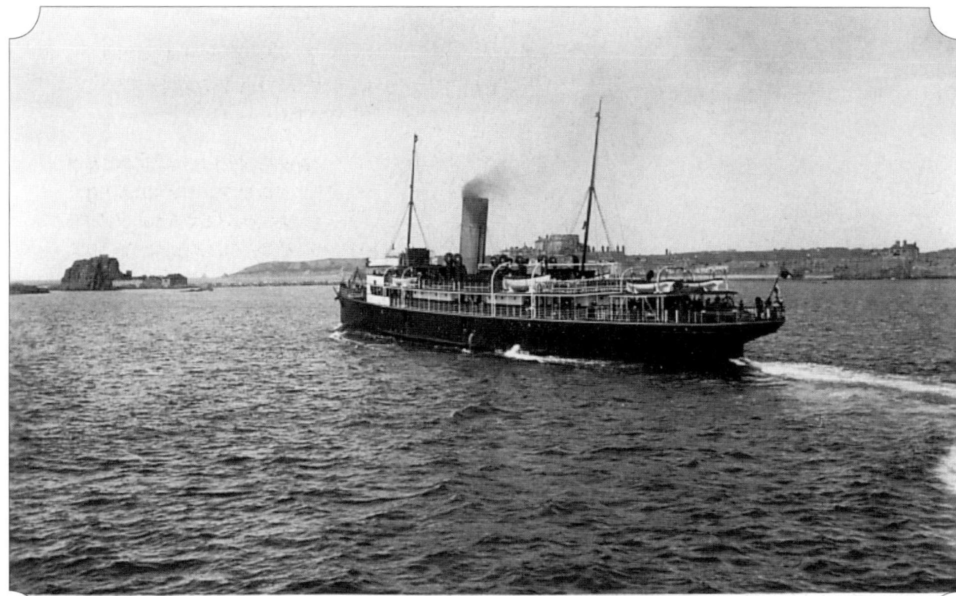

Dear Mum & Dad
I was sick as a dog on the way over but it is great here now. There is some fine wine I can bring you back for a present.
From Harry

~

Eight words say it all:

'Arrived well
Safe trip
Not sick
Weather grand'

S.S. *Alberta* heading past Elizabeth Castle breakwater and out to sea. This twin-screw steamer was launched in 1900 and sold in 1930, no doubt replaced by the new generation of ships like S.S. *Isle of Guernsey* pictured opposite.

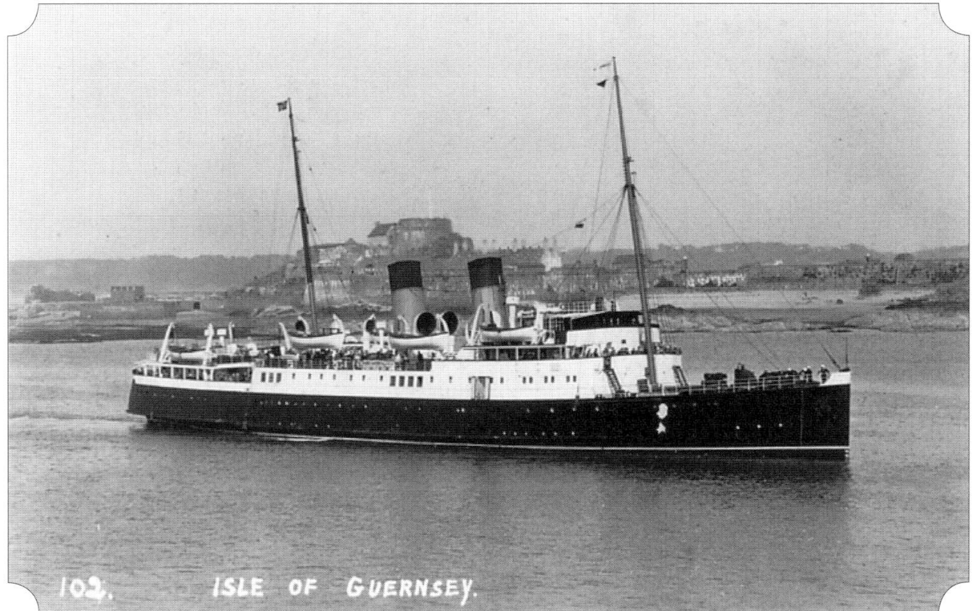

S.S. *Isle of Guernsey* making its careful approach past Elizabeth Castle to reach the harbour. This vessel, together with its sister ships the *Isle of Jersey* and the *Isle of Sark*, entered service in the early 1930s and served the islands for the following three decades.

A postcard message sent in 1951 to Miss Ross in Grimsby:

'Well we have arrived safely after a very good crossing. There are quite a few young people staying but some are most peculiar!! Yesterday was heavenly, we spent the afternoon in & out of the sea listening to the cricket.
Cheerio, Alice Walker'

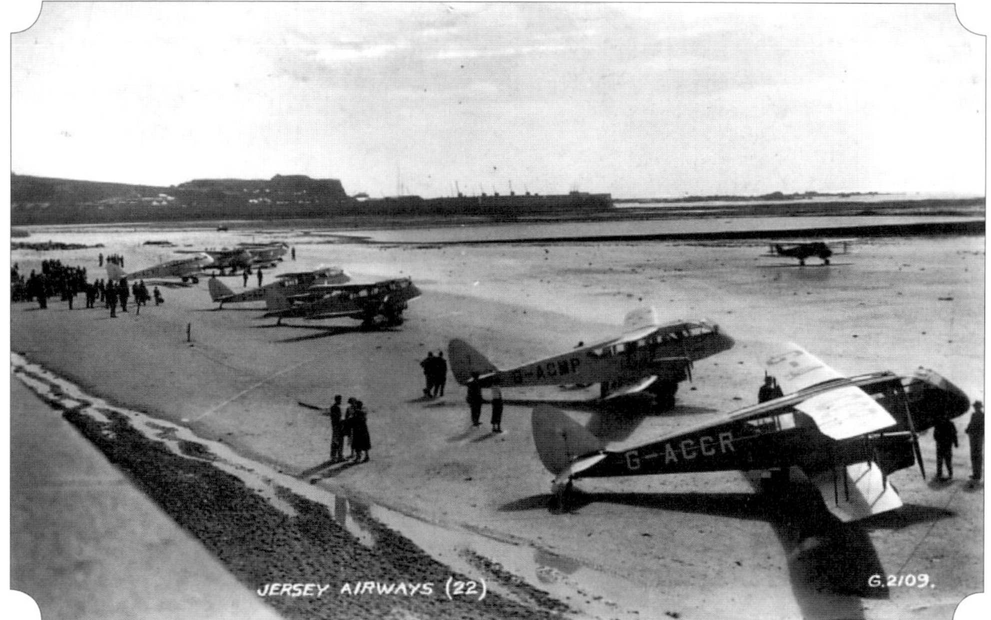

A postcard message sent in 1934, in the days when planes landed on the beach at West Park:

'Dear Mother,
Arrived OK. If you think of coming take my tip come by air.
Yours Bill'

~

Another message, this one sent in 1937:

'Having a lovely time. Flying is great. Only 3 hours from door to door.'

Jersey Airport – see opposite – was opened in 1937 but, from 1933, passenger aircraft flying from England landed and took off from the beach at West Park which, of course, depended upon the state of the tide. This postcard view shows a number of Dragon Rapides, a twin-propellor biplane.

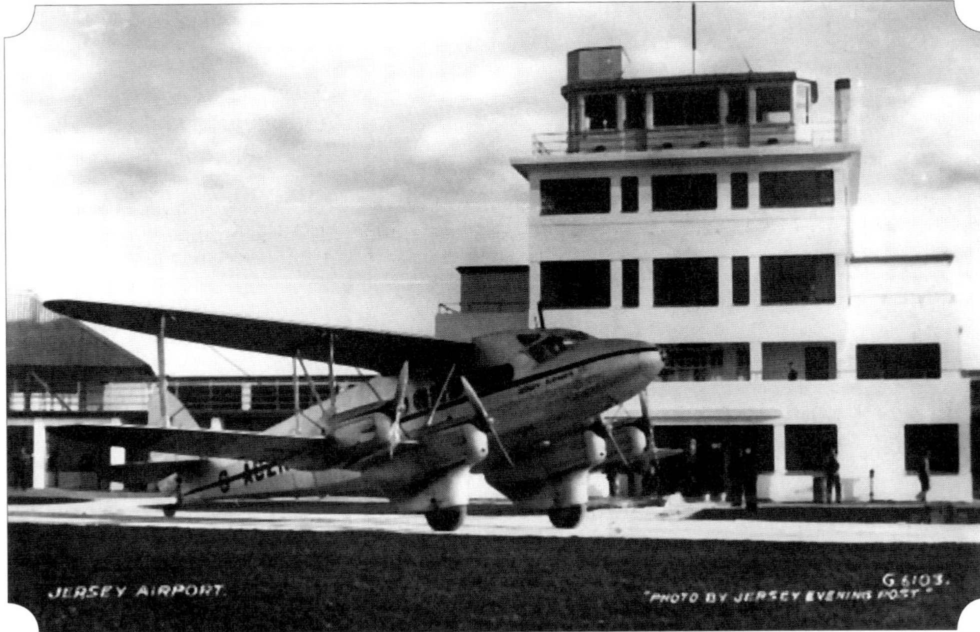

Dragon Rapide at Jersey Airport. This view gives a good impression of the original airport building, with its attractive wedding cake structure supporting the control tower at its summit.

This card is postmarked 14th August, 1939, and is addressed to Mrs Keech of Battersea, London. The sender's message reads:

'Dear Mum
Arrived here 10.30am having caught 9 o'clock 'plane from Southampton. Flew in beautiful weather - quite an experience. Hope everything is well.
Love, Charles'

~

Another message, this time sent in 1952, reads:

'Dear Elfrida
We enjoyed our first flight and found it a most comfortable journey only 1½ hours from Northolt... The weather is very good and we are enjoying our holiday here very much.'

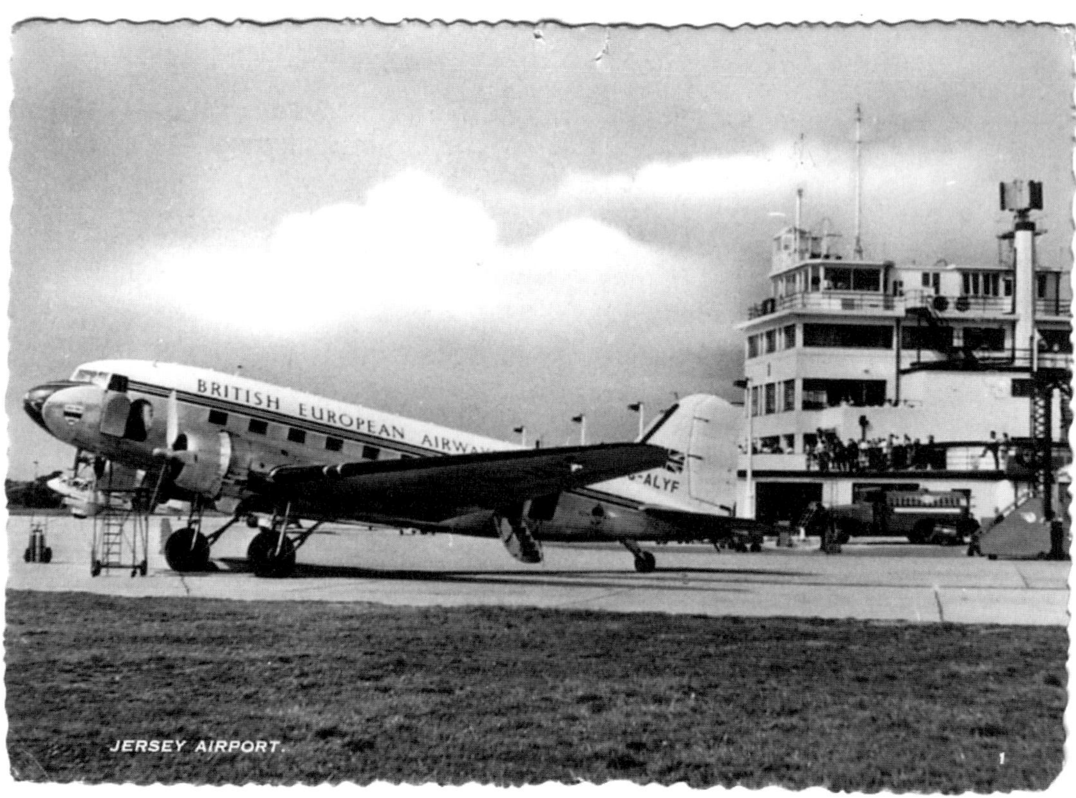

The message on this card:

'This is the type of plane* we came here in. Good job it wasn't yesterday, the weather grounded them for most of the day. Apparently it has been a bad season altogether, and the locals don't promise anything better. Today the sky is overcast, and there is a rougher sea running, quite a picture really. The hotel is quite good, clean, and the food well cooked.

Love, Vera.'

* [Dakota DC3]

~ Where to Stay ~

An advertisement for the Royal Yacht Hotel in the 1920s claimed it to be 'The Oldest Established Hotel in the Island ... Facing Sea and Harbour, and Most Centrally Situated for Railway Stations', and that 'Excursion Cars start from Hotel Twice Daily during the Season; Hotel Omnibus Meets Mail Boats'.

Many of the earliest hotels were, unsurprisingly, situated close to the harbour. All the larger establishments provided excursion cars and met new arrivals at the quay.

The opening of hotels and boarding houses, some purpose-built but others converted from older buildings, facilitated the development of tourism from the early 19th century onwards.

Every establishment sought to advertise its own unique features, sometimes with a little exaggeration. St Brelade's Bay Hotel claimed that: 'This is the only Hotel in the Channel Islands affording facilities for Sea Bathing, which may be enjoyed at any state of the tide from Sands in front of the house.' The Stag's Head Hotel, at Snow Hill, a busy intersection, was 'Centrally Situated. Every Room in Front of House with outlook down Main Street of Town'. And the Halkett Hotel: 'Visitors arriving at the Height of the Season and desiring a degree of quietude [more or less unobtainable in some parts of the Town just then] can be assured of finding it at this Establishment'.

There have long been as many hotels outside St Helier as within, though many of the largest have been in town. Between the wars hotels began to offer the attractions of a swimming pool, a billiards room, a ping pong room, a London Dance Band and Cabaret, 'Young Company' and 'Small Tables' (as opposed to tables shared with other guests).

Holiday Camps first appeared in the 1920s but both those at Portelet and Plémont are long gone.

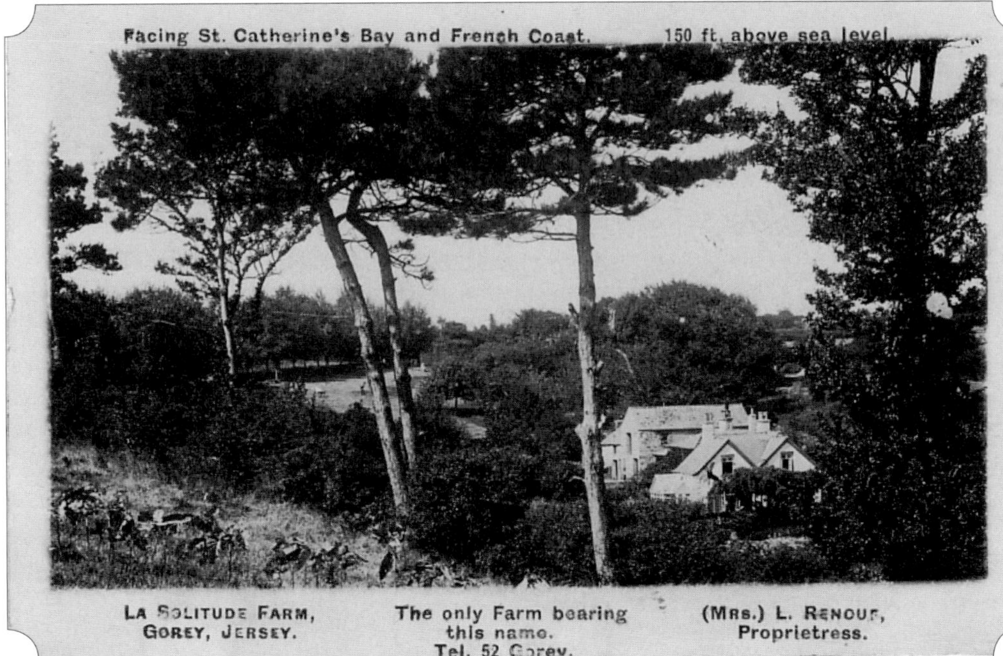

This card was postmakred 27th July, 1903 and its message reads:

'Arrived here safely. It is an ideal spot. We can look right over to France from our bedroom window. I am writing this by the sea. It is just nice, not too hot. There are 35 people in the house - 2 French families. A good many sleep in a large house on the hill and in some cottages all belonging to the proprietress. I am glad we are in the house - our bedroom is the window next to which I have put a cross, Drawing room underneath. They make up parties for excursions from the house. I think it's going to be very nice.

N.

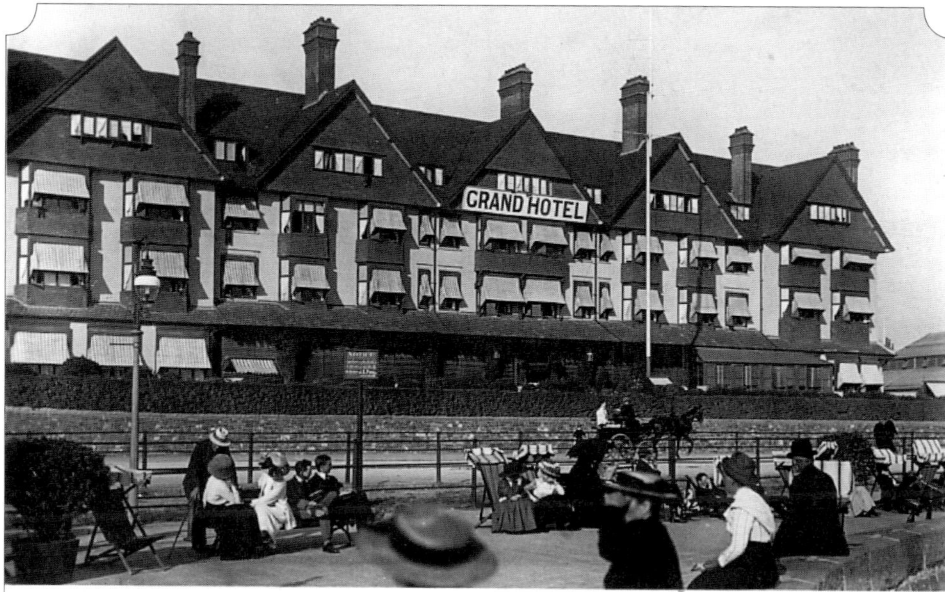

This Edwardian view from the top of the former slipway opposite the Grand shows its windows well protected with stripy blinds. The railings behind the seated holidaymakers enclose the railway track which ran to St Aubin and beyond. The upmarket Grand, with its views across St Aubin's Bay, was commandeered by the Germans during the Occupation.

Message sent in 1926:

'We had a gorgeous day for our crossing, though I did succomb once. The house is in a lovely position, high on a windy hill overlooking St Aubin's Bay.
9 planes have just arrived on beach below us and returned to England.

~

Message written on 1st August, 1952:

'Having a very good holiday here. Saw the Battle of Flowers yesterday and it was marvellous. Everything parched as they have had very little rain since April'

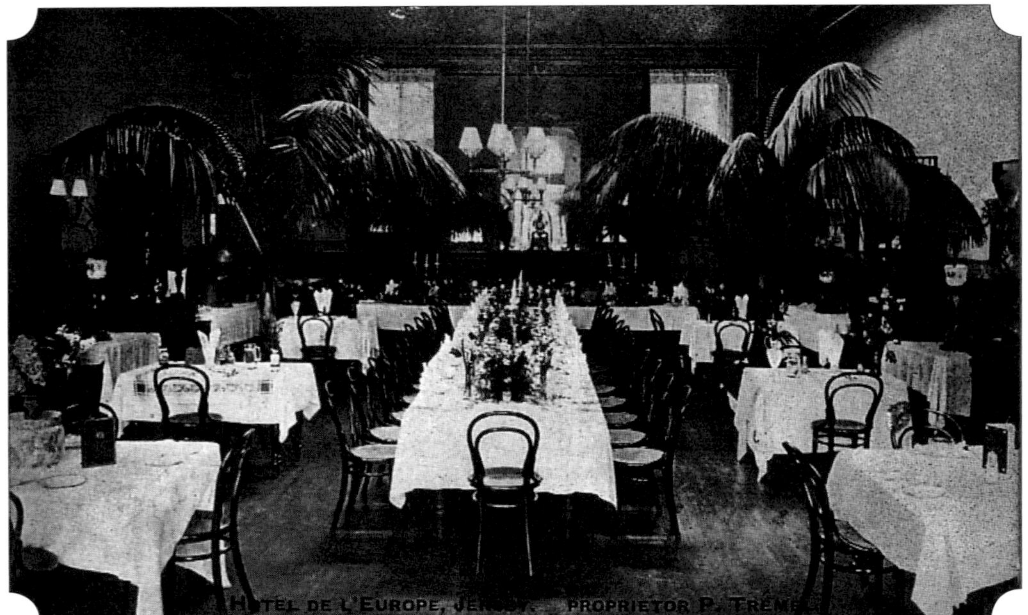

The impressive dining room at Hotel de L'Europe boasted an impressive dining room with a fine display of palms and a mix of seating arrangements, some communal and others separate.

Message written on 1st August, 1952:

'Dear Vi,
We are still having a wonderful time and just can't believe the weather. Every day has been hot & sunny. We are sitting here outside a little café overlooking Portelet Sands - you could never imagine such blue sea & sky or such golden sands. Are going to swim again this afternoon - this is the life! Helen very impressed with Jersey. We are going on an island tour next Thursday.

Joan'

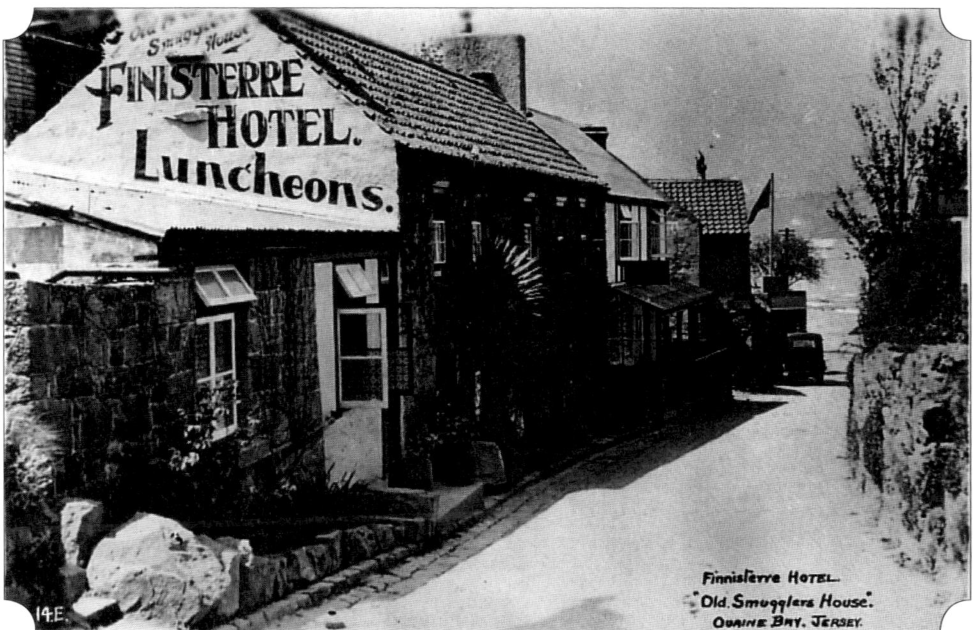

The Finisterre Hotel at the foot of Ouaisné Hill, now known as the Smugglers Inn, leading to the slipway and a fine beach.

Message from 1910:

We are having a grand time here the weather is lovely. I dread coming back to London again I hope you are all well. I have not heard from anyone at home since I've been here.. Love from Lance and your loving sister Esther.'

~

From 1936:

'Had a good crossing over children very good. Weather is dull but not wet, food is first class so why worry.

Best wishes HM'

~

And from 1937:

'Arrived here Saturday morning feeling like death after a foul trip. Weather not too good so far, hotel quite nice.

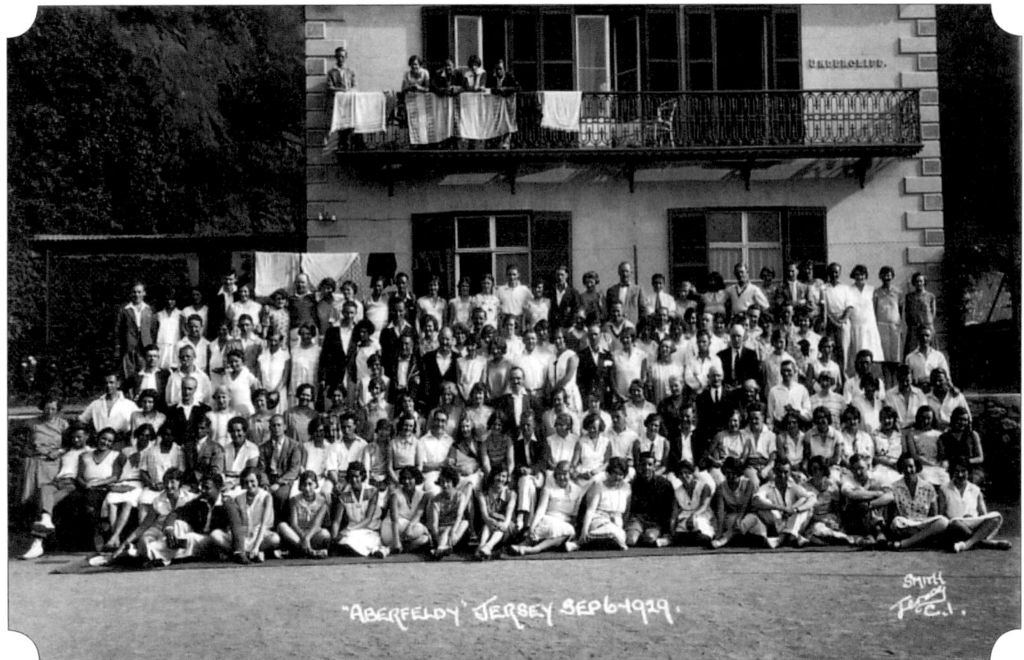

An impressive gathering of guests at the Aberfeldy, 6th September, 1929. The Aberfeldy, in Old St John's Road, was a large hotel which has since been redeveloped as luxury apartments known as Park Heights.

Message to Mr & Mrs Hayward of Freshwater, Isle of Wight:

'Dear Mum & Dad
Arrived safely in Jersey after a really wizard journey. Lovely weather on arrival. Passed over IOW. I saw your striped dress.
Love in haste, Bob & Marion'

~

And from 1953:

Dear Phylis
We have got some very exciting company on the same table.
Best wishes Rita'

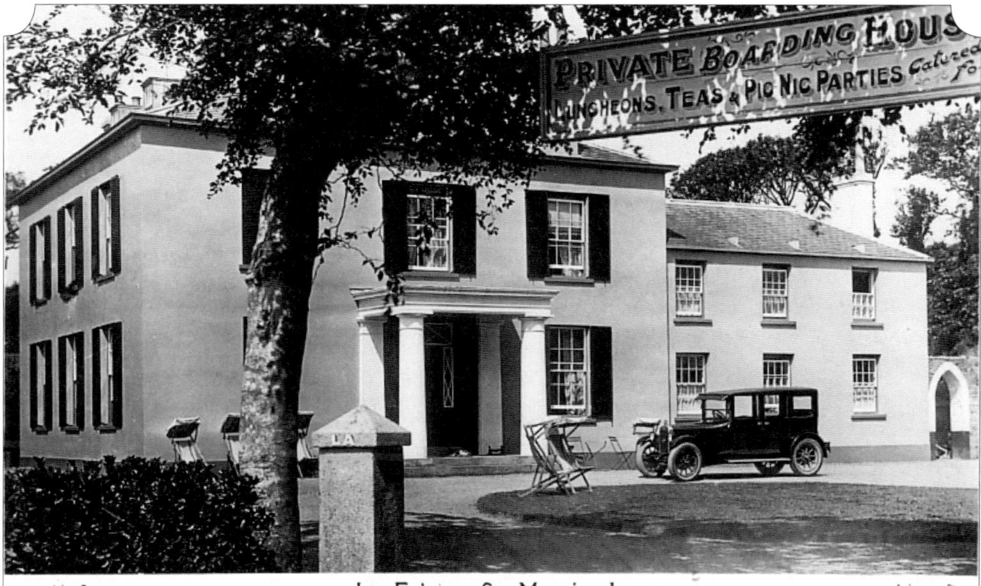

The notice overhead reads: 'Private Boarding House; Luncheons; Teas & Pic Nic Parties Catered for.

This card is postmarked 20th July 1932 and its message reads:

'To-day we came over to Jersey. The picture is the hotel at which we had lunch on our way round the island.'

~

Message to Mr Pipe of Hornsey, London, in 1913:

'We had a very rough crossing coming over and I got a nasty cut on the leg, but we are doing alright now.

Fred'

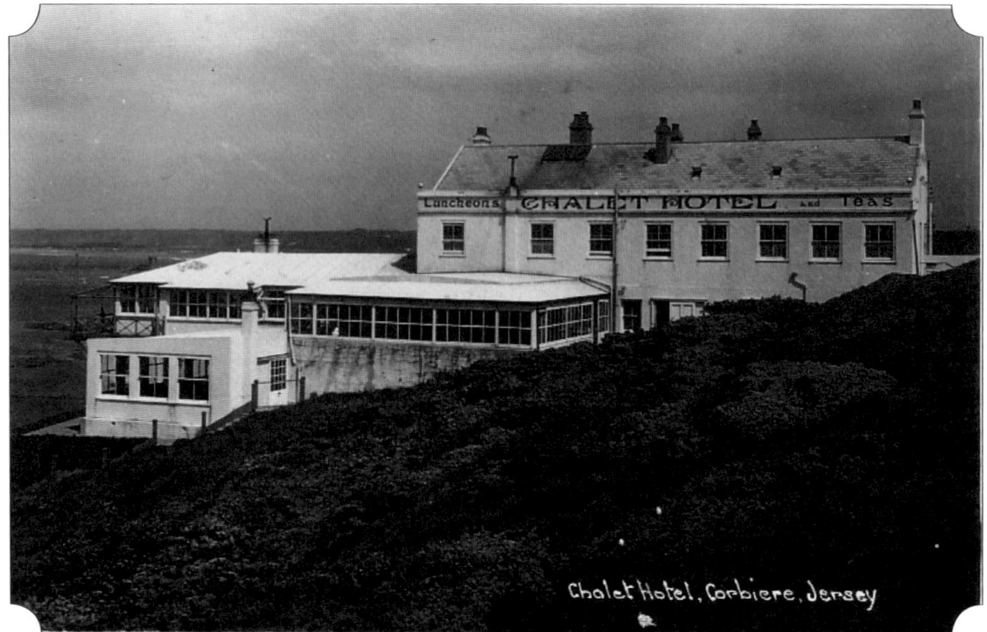

'Hotel de France
St Saviour's Road
I would like to thank you for the arrangements you made to enable my friend & I to have such an enjoyable holiday. Jersey is everything I hoped it would be lovely beaches, a fine shopping centre and a very friendly pleasant hotel. Anybody coming to Hotel de France can be assured of a very enjoyable vacation. The journey over was very rough & my friend was ill but I was able to brave the storm. I do hope you had a good holiday. I am determined to return to Jersey sometime, but would fly next time.
Kind regards
Jean Windsor'

From an advertisement for the Chalet Hotel at Corbière in 1937: 'Stands in Own Grounds of 8 acres. Within 2 mins. of Bus and Railway Station, one mile Aerodrome, Sea Bathing from Hotel, Cheerful dining-room, Separate Tables. Own Farm Produce. Near 18-hole Golf Links. Tennis Court. Garage.

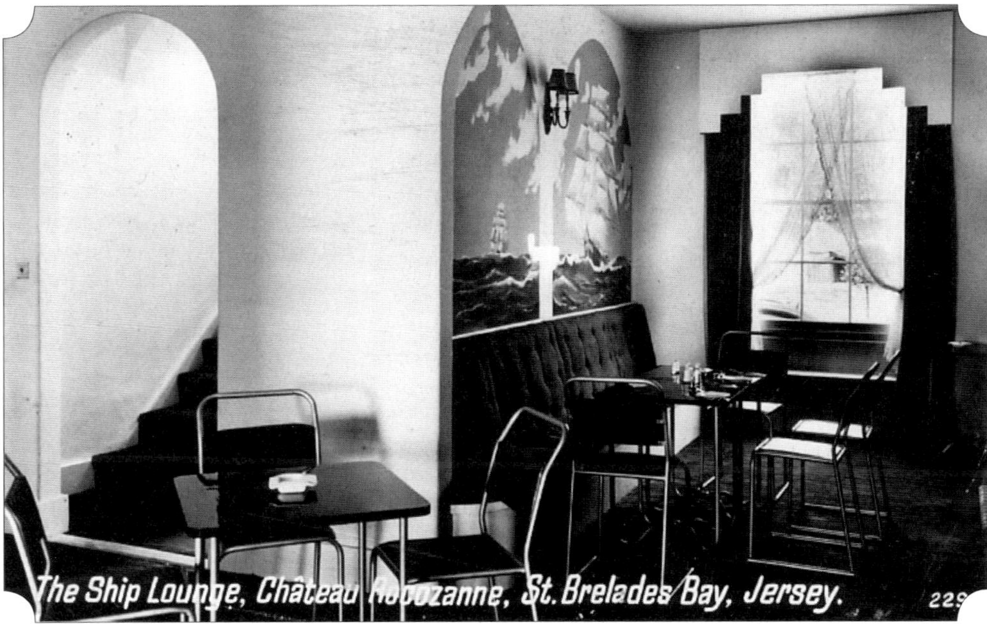

Chateau Rocozanne is described in an advertisement in 1965 as 'a small, select hotel with the sea at the bottom of the garden'. The interior is uncompromisingly modern, with tubular steel chairs and tables and clean lines everywhere.

'I wish you were here. We are having a lovely time. There are heaps of nice people here. Are you away on your holidays. We shall not be home for a month yet. Write if you have time. Be good.

Best love, Maude.'

~

Message from a card post-marked 4th September, 1919 and addressed to Mr & Mrs Ford of Sherborne, Dorset:

'Dear Papa & Blanche,
Just a line to let you know all's well. Have had a good time here and feel much better. Returning to Dorchester by Saturday's boat. The crossings have been pretty rough lately.

Love Charlie'

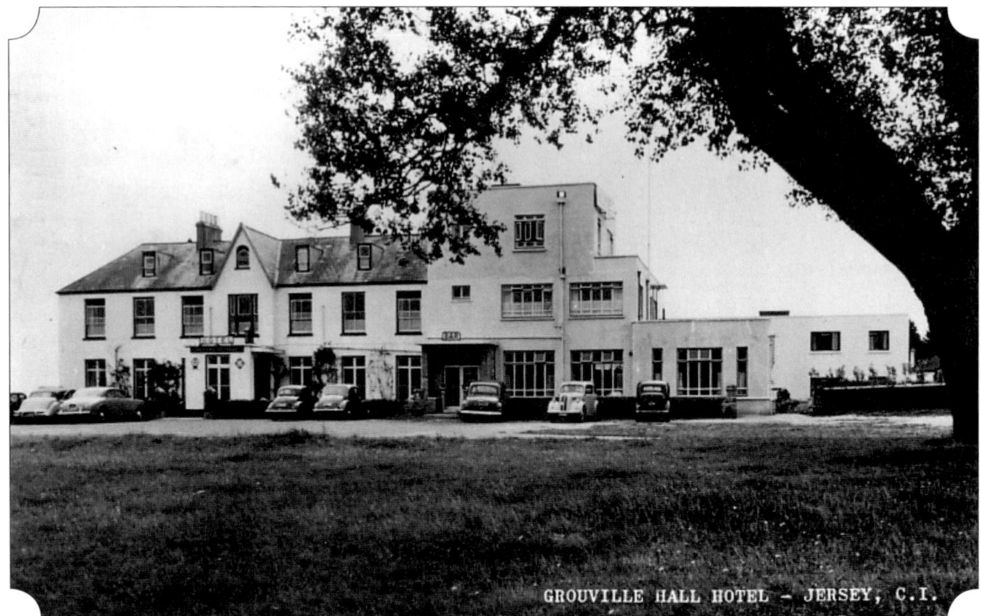

'Well my dear I feel very sad that instead of coming to see you and young Hugh I have had to come here with so little time to spare. It was Hobson's Choice as if I had stayed until I sail for California in January I would have to pay the whole of 1958 income tax which will pay my fare to America. Hope to see you when I get back.'

Grouville Hall Hotel: All the cars parked in front are Bristish makes, and note the AA and RAC plaques either side of the entrance porch. This card is postmarked 24th November, 1958 and its message – see right – makes interesting reading.

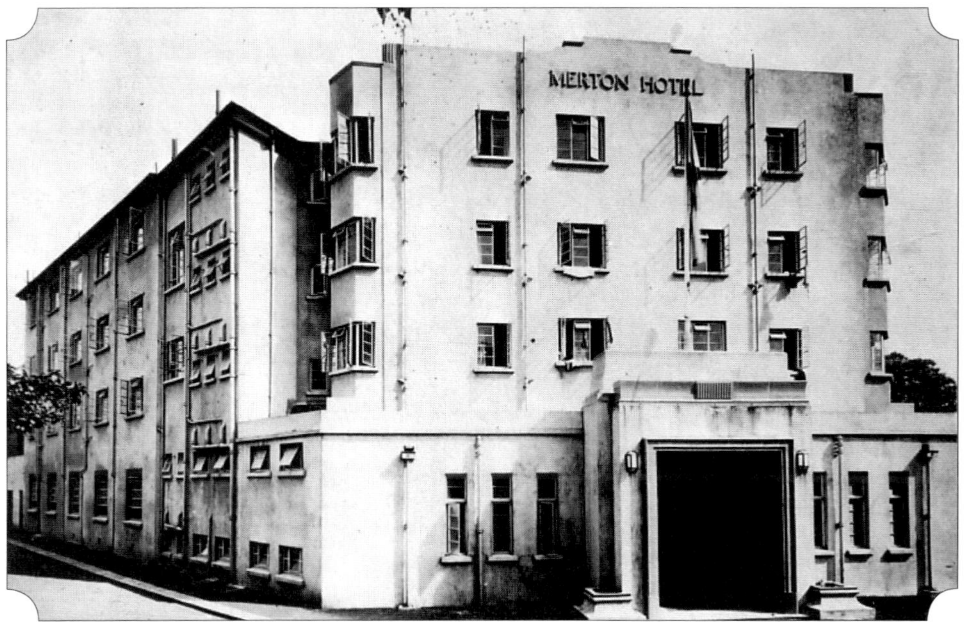

Message on card postmarked 1947 and sent to Nottingham:

'Merton Hotel, Jersey
Having a grand time weather and everything ideal. 500 staying at this hotel plenty of life had a lovely crossing should like to stay here.
Love Doris'

Looking rather bleak in this view, the Merton Hotel has a huge capacity. An advertisement from 1955 states that it is the largest hotel in the Channel Islands, accommodating 550 guests.

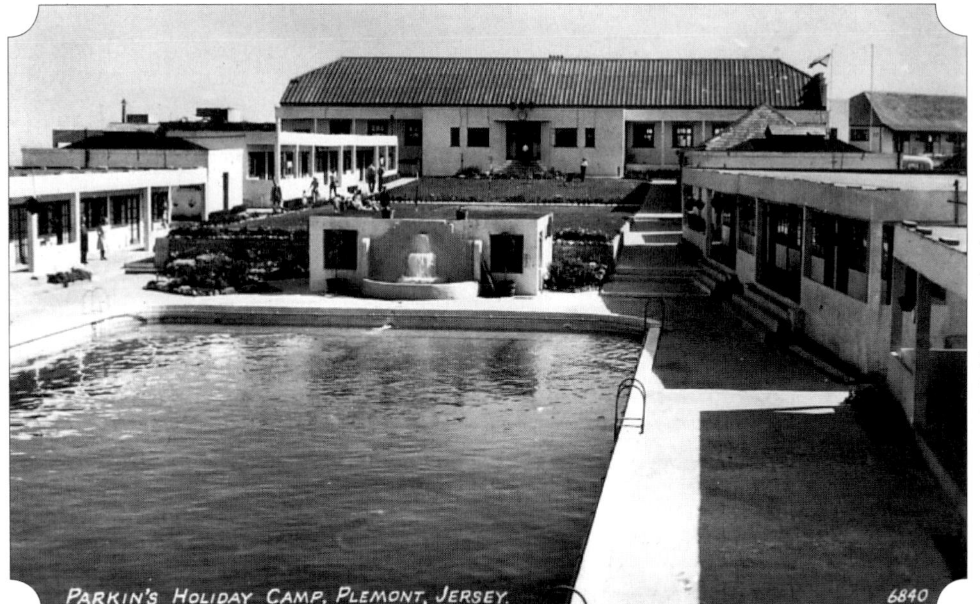
PARKIN'S HOLIDAY CAMP, PLEMONT, JERSEY. 6840

Message from card sent to E L Nicholls of Portsmouth:

'Parkins Holiday Camp
Plemont

Dear Mum
Arrived after exciting journey saw fire near Southampton, stopped by fog & arrived 4.45 in morning but had breakfast on board and left at 6.30. Having grand time. Everything cheap even bought you a bottle of Eau de Cologne for £7.11.2d what is 15s there. Coming home Sunday morning.

Keith'

The holiday camp offered a new kind of holidat experience, ideally suited to families with children. The accommodation was fairly basic but there was plenty of scope for healthy activities and for getting together with fellow holidaymakers. Parkin's, later Pontin's, has been closed and abandoned for many years and the site, which many say should not have been developed in the first place and should now be left to revert to nature, awaits its fate.

~ Getting About ~

For such a small island, Jersey has a remarkable network of roads – around 600 miles in total. This is partly thanks to General Don, Lieutenant-Governor of Jersey during the Napoleonic Period. Though built originally for military purposes, these highways have been of benefit to locals and tourists alike in their movement around the island whether travelling by car, bus, motor coach or bicycle.

1870 witnessed the advent of rail transport with the opening of the line from the Weighbridge in St Helier to St Aubin, and its extension, in 1884, to Corbière. The stations en route were First Tower, Millbrook, Bel Royal, Beaumont, La Haule, St Aubin, Pont Marquet, Don Bridge, Blanches Banques (for La Moye Golf Links) and La Moye. The Jersey Eastern Railway, opened in 1873, ran from Snow Hill to Gorey via St Luke's, Grève d'Azette, Samarès, Le Hocq, Pontac, La Rocque, Fauvic, Grouville and Gorey Village. At one time it was possible to purchase a through ticket from St Helier to Paris, via a boat link between Gorey and Carteret in Normandy.

Both rail lines closed before the war, in 1936 and 1929 respectively. Motor bus services began in 1910 though initially used in conjunction with the railways. For example, to get to Grève de Lecq or Plémont, you would catch the train to Beaumont, then catch the bus. From its peak in the mid-1920s, railway traffic steadily declined in the face of competition from buses and private cars.

Jersey Motor Transport, 'the JMT', and currently, Liberty Bus, provide a comprehensive network of routes to all parts of the island from a state-of-the-art bus station in St Helier. Visitors may also hire cars, scooters and bicycles; the once popular coach tours are still available, though there are far fewer companies than during their heyday in the 1950s and '60s.

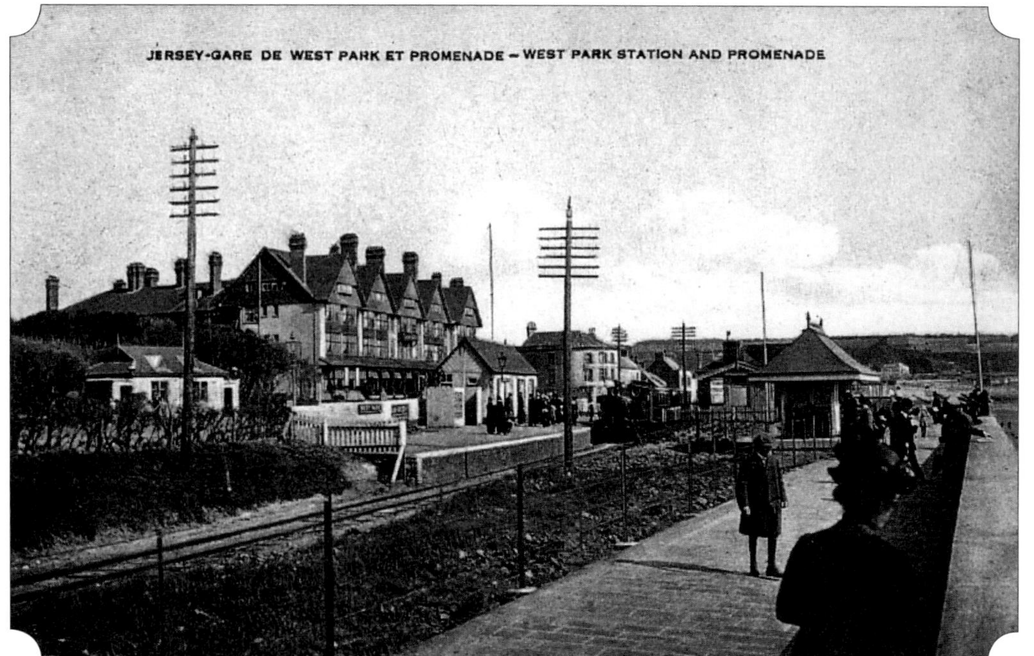

Message from a card postmarked 1907:

'Wilfred and I have had a splendid drive this afternoon to the quarries near Devil's Hole, the weather is now splendid although it did not clear until nearly nine o'clock this morning having rained all night.
We have arranged to visit La Rocque on Friday afternoon will probably go by the 2 o'clock Train.'

West Park Station with train arriving. This was the first stop on the line west from the Weighbridge to St Aubin. The public conveniences, on the left, at the entrance to Victoria Park are visible, as is the shelter beside the promenade and the impressive five-gabled Grand Hotel.

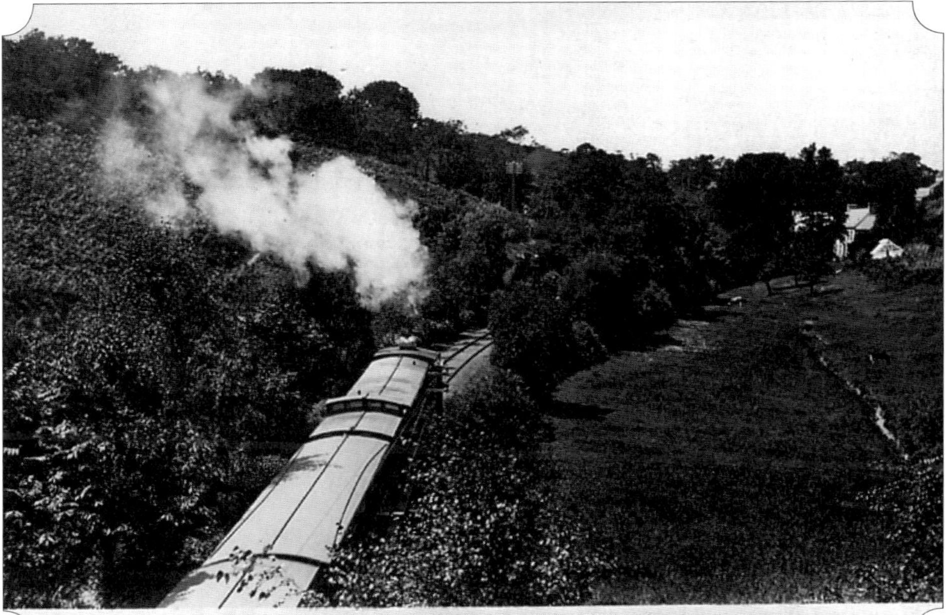

VIEW ON WESTERN RAILWAY, ST. HELIER'S TO CORBIERE, JERSEY. No. 21.

A train chugging its way to Corbiére soon after leaving St Aubin. This wonderfully evocative view is taken from the road bridge across the line before its closure in 1936.

Message on card postmarked 6 July 1928 and sent to E J Cockshott Esq., c/o The Safety Engineer, Post Office Engineeriing Dept, Bristol:

'at Aberfeldy St heliers

Dear Mr Cockshott

We are having a glorious holiday. Heaps of sunshine, sometimes 14-15 hrs a day. Am almost a Red Indian. Expect to come back thoroughly fit & help to shove things along.

KR'

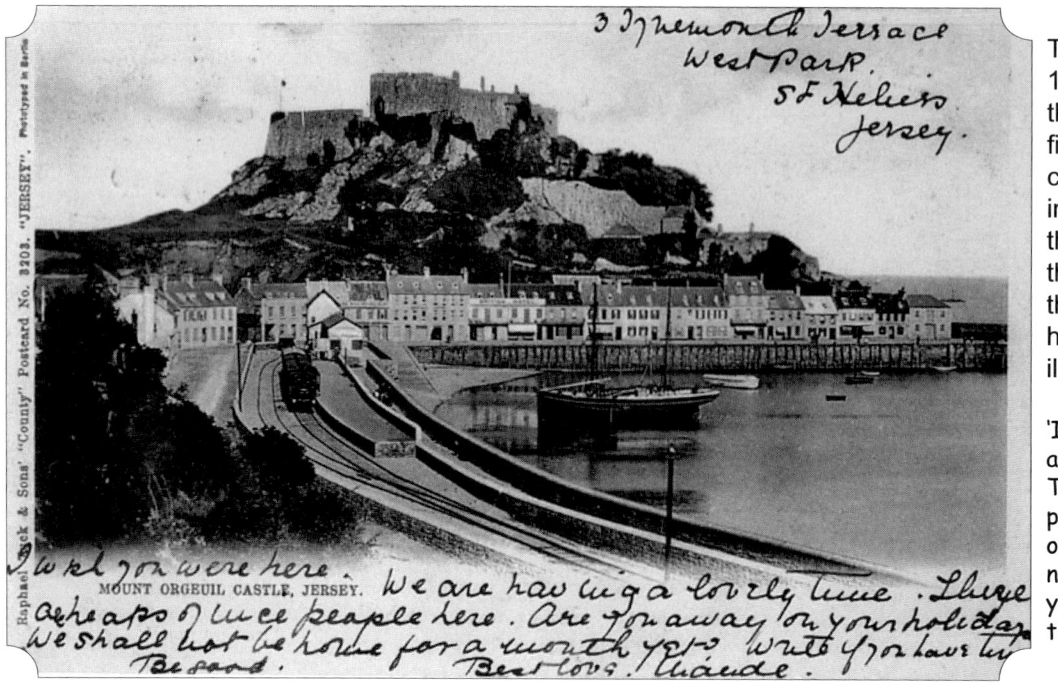

Train at Gorey Station, the terminus of the Jersey Eastern Railway.

This card is postmarked 10th August, 1902, the year it was first permitted for correspondents to include a message on the card's address side, though in this case the sender confined her message to the illustration:

'I wish you were here. We are having a lovely time. There are heaps of nice people here. Are you away on your holidays. We shall not be home for a month yet. Write if you have time. Be good.

Best love, Maude'

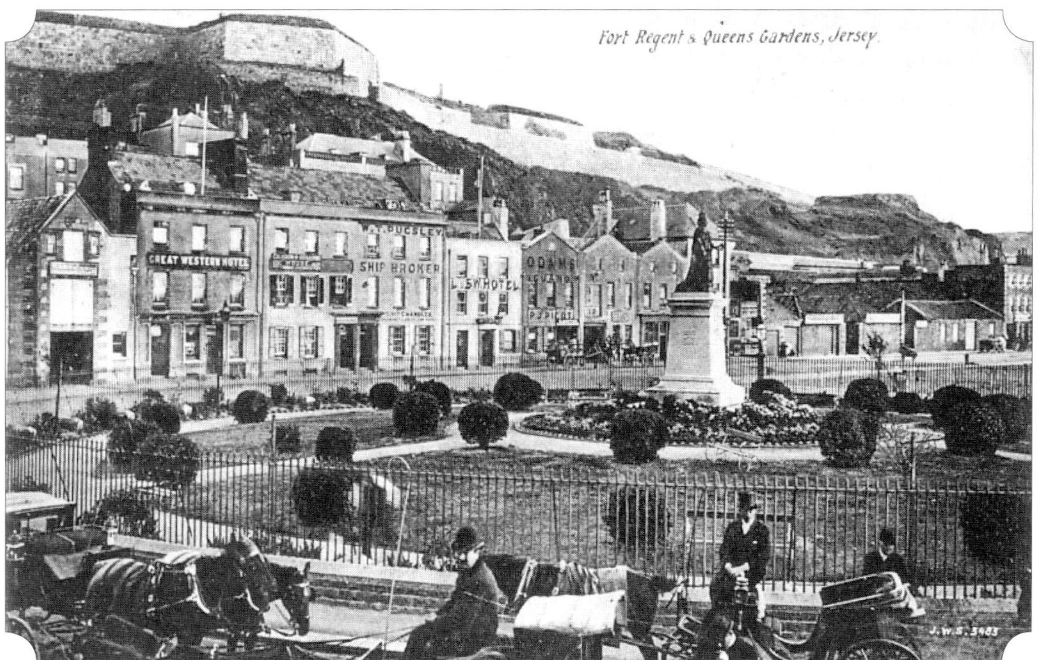

Horse-drawn taxi cabs awaiting fares at Queen's Gardens (now Liberation Square). Note the hotels beyond: the Great Western Hotel (now the Ha'penny Bridge pub, and the L & SW (London & South-Western) Hotel, centre – the two rival railway companies which operated passenger boats to and from Jersey.

Message on undated postcard:

'Dear Mr Leman
The weather has changed over here now, but the first five days were grand. We have been on some lovely coach rides round the island. Beautiful scenery. We really enjoyed ourselves but shall not be sorry to be back in good old England.

Mrs Parkinson'

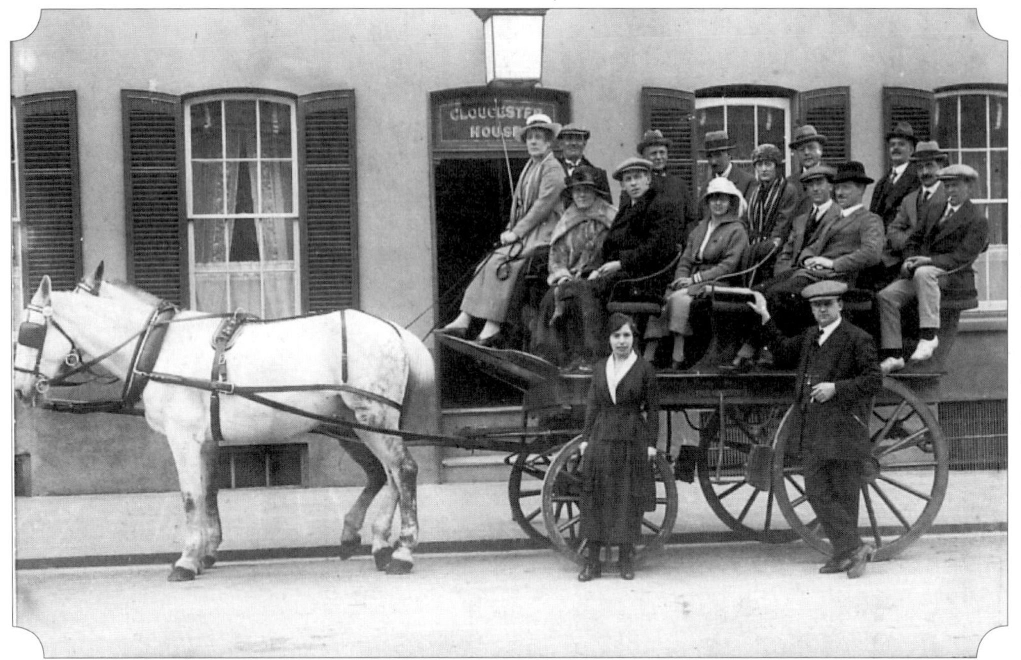

A well laden horse-drawn carriage. Like the hotel group phptpgraph on page 22, this picture of holidaymakers about to set off (presumably on a tour of the island) was taken to be offered for sale to the folk pictured.

From a Guide Book published in 1902:

'There are several livery stables each have their own stereotyped rounds, which are announced in the hotels the night before. Fare 2s.6d. a head. The cars call at the hotels, and the lodgings if required. A tip for the guide, whose information must not always be trusted.'

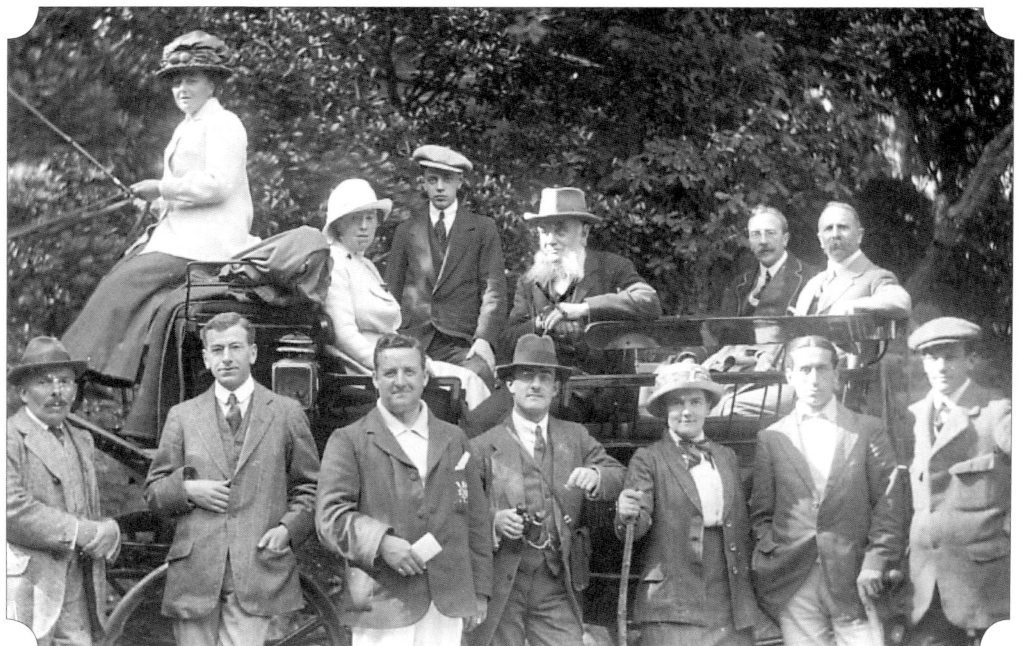

This card is postmarked 25th September 1915. The message reads:

'Dear Ma
What do you think of this taken of our party yesterday at Prince's Tower, the highest point in the Island. The lady with the white hat in the break and I constitute the Poly. party. Don't you think this rather good of Sonny [the heavily whiskered gent in the centre]
Love from George.'

A carefully posed group photograph taken during an outing to Prince's Tower. Until it was demolished in 1924, the Tower offered long reaching views over the island and was a magnet for visitors. The much more ancient dolmen beneath the mound on which the Tower was erected in the late 18th century is today a major attraction.

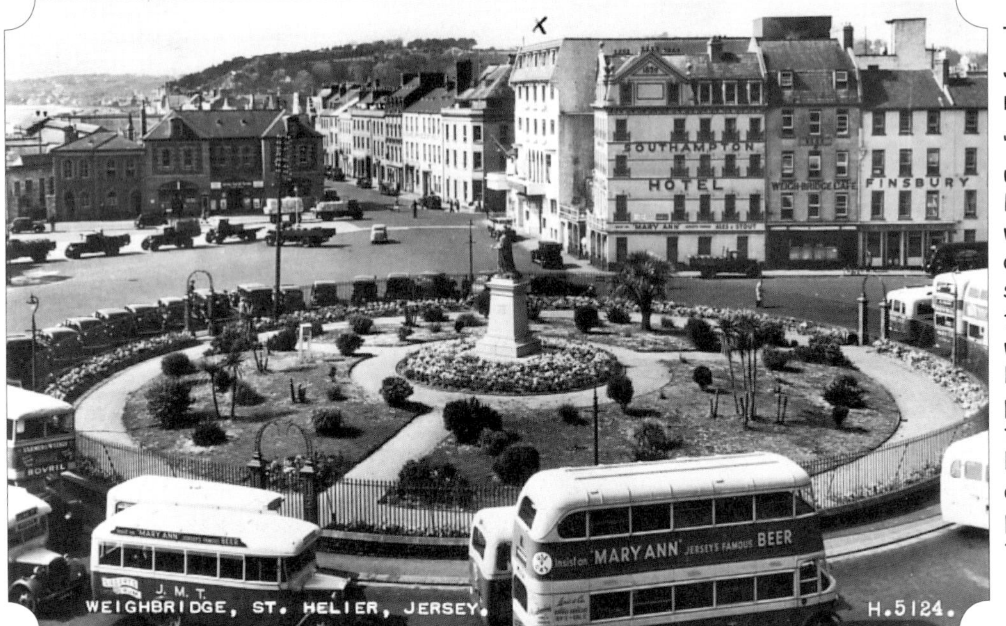

This card is postmarked 5th June, 1954; the message reads:

'Dear Pop. Writing this high up the cliffs looking out to Bouley Bay. It's a wee bit warmer today - but we still are wearing our top coats - no sign of sun. The cross on the front marks the Hotel where we are staying [The Pomme D'Or]. Glad you went to the pictures & you are OK. Sorry to hear about Mr Wilkins - he hadn't looked strong to me for a while now. Give my Babe a pat. What size collar does she take? Please.

Love, Irene XX'

Weighbridge, St Helier (now Liberation Square) showing JMT (Jersey Motor Transport) buses, including double-deckers. Motor taxis are lined up on the far side. Also visible are potato lorries queueing for the weighbridge. Queen's Gardens were eventually cleared to allow the expansion of the bus station.

~ St Helier ~

'A large Harbour; a maze of streets, busy and prosperous, but noted for their cleanliness; a huge fort rising perpendicularly above the town; good shops; numerous places of worship; a miscellaneous assortment of carriages and well-appointed "Jersey cars", plus a general air of comfort and well-being, are the prominent features of St Helier.' This was the description of the town from a guide book published between the wars.

St Helier was the place where many visitors stayed, in hotels or boarding house. Even if they did not stay in town, it was where most of them did their shopping before returning home. Today most of the shops are, regrettably, the same shops as in any High Street on the mainland, though a few of the largest are still Jersey concerns and retain their individual character. In the 1920s, Voisin's of King Street advertised themselves as 'General Drapers, Outfitters, Complete House Furnishers and Confectioners'.

De Gruchy's, just yards away, was 'The Oldest and Largest Drapery Establishment in the Channel Islands; Established 1810', and were 'General Drapers and House Furnishers. High-Class Tailors and Outfitters, Hosiers, Hatters, etc., Milliners, Dressmakers and Ladies' Tailors.'

Owing to Jersey's former tax-free status, visitors were tempted to buy goods which were more expensive on the mainland. These included perfumes; Jersey Eau de Cologne was manufactured by Larbalestier, Luce, Dubras and De Faye (by Royal Appointment). Alcohol and tobacco were the other main staples of the duty-free trade. The local cigarette company, Ching & Co., promised that their Navy Cut Cigarettes 'will add the last touch of enjoyment to your Holidays'; they were 6d. a pack of 20 before the war.

Aside from shopping opportunities, 'In addition to its convenience as a centre, the town is lively with evening entertainments'.

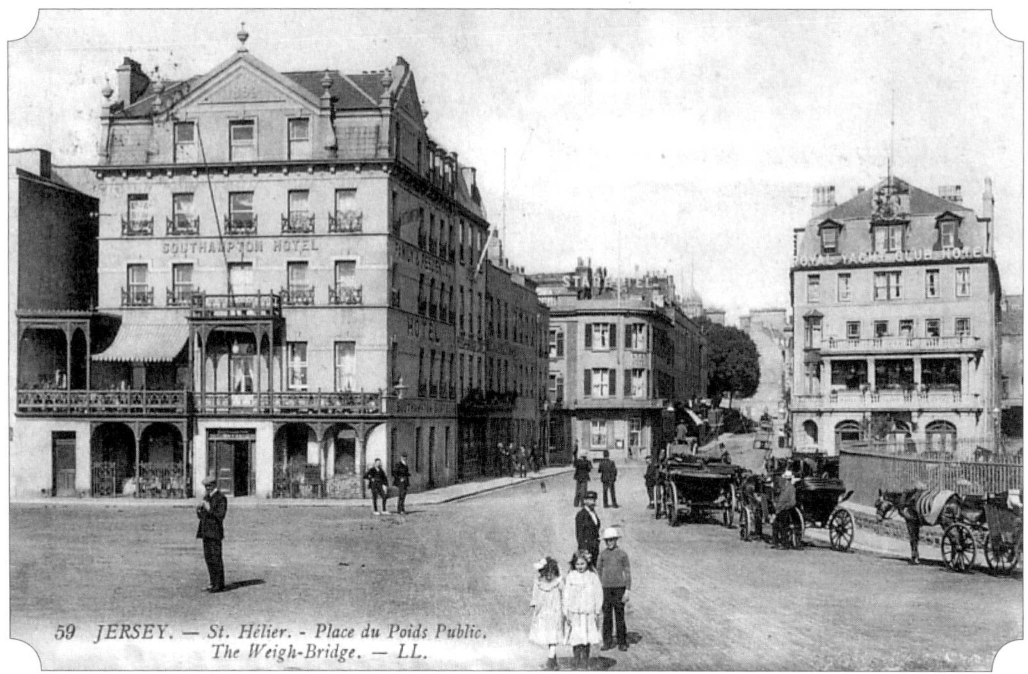

Message sent to Miss Emery of Bromley, Kent:

'Dear Sylvia,
Just a note to say I arrived alright, just in time for lunch! - at 12.20 to be precise. The weather is much too good to be true but here's hoping that it stays the way it is now - or possibly a little cooler. It seems as if I am staying at one of the best places in town - so I should do alright - especially with cigarettes at 1/6 for 20. What I have seen of the scenery seems to be worth looking at & there are no crowds, even in St Helier on a Saturday!

Love Ted

This Edwardian view along Mulcaster Street near its junction with The Esplanade is still easily recognisable and would have been the first sight of St Helier to greet visitors arriving at the Harbour. This card is postmarked 24th July, 1909.

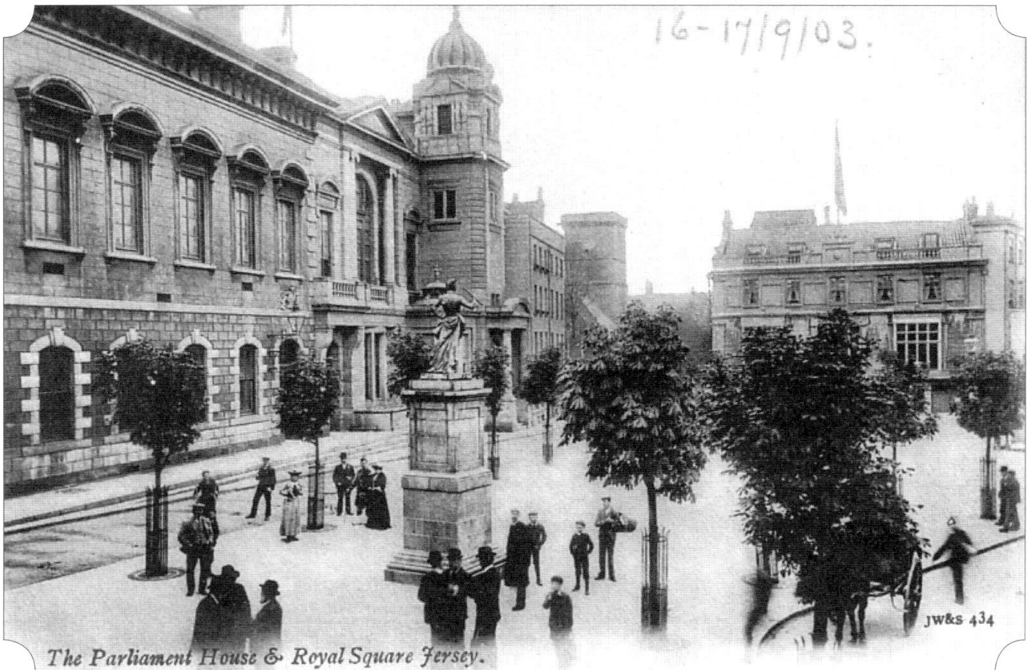

This card captions the view as 'The Parliament & Royal Square' and is dated 1903. The horse chestnut trees were planted in 1894, hence their small stature. The Parliament House is more usually known as the States Chambers. It was formerly the Market Square and the site where the Battle of Jersey was won in 1781.

The Royal Square is where important announcements are made, most notably on Liberation Day, 1945. The Royal Square can fairly be described as the heart of St Helier and, therefore, of the island. The tower of the Town Church can be seen in the middle distance. The statue of King George II, masquerading as a Roman Emperor, originally erected in 1751, has witnessed many changes over the past two and a half centuries; his presence there gave rise to the saying, 'There's only one good man in Jersey and he's in the Royal Square'.

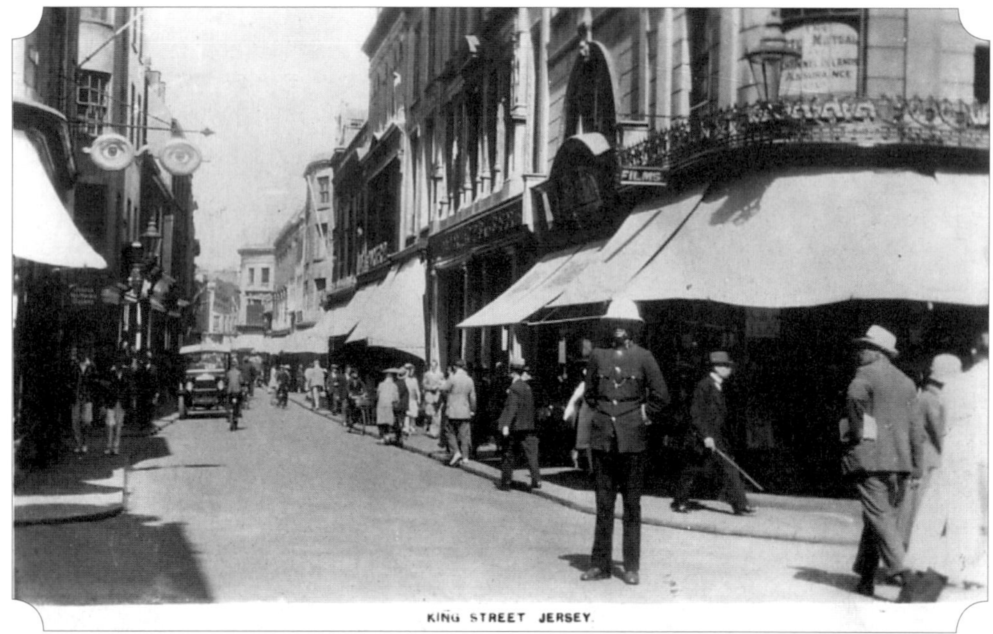

Junction of King Street and Halkett Place

This card is not postmarked but was most likely sent between the wars. The message reads:

'This place is by no means a one horse town, it has its traffic problems as well as any other although to look at the policmen and the helmets they wear you'd think they were in India.

Albert'

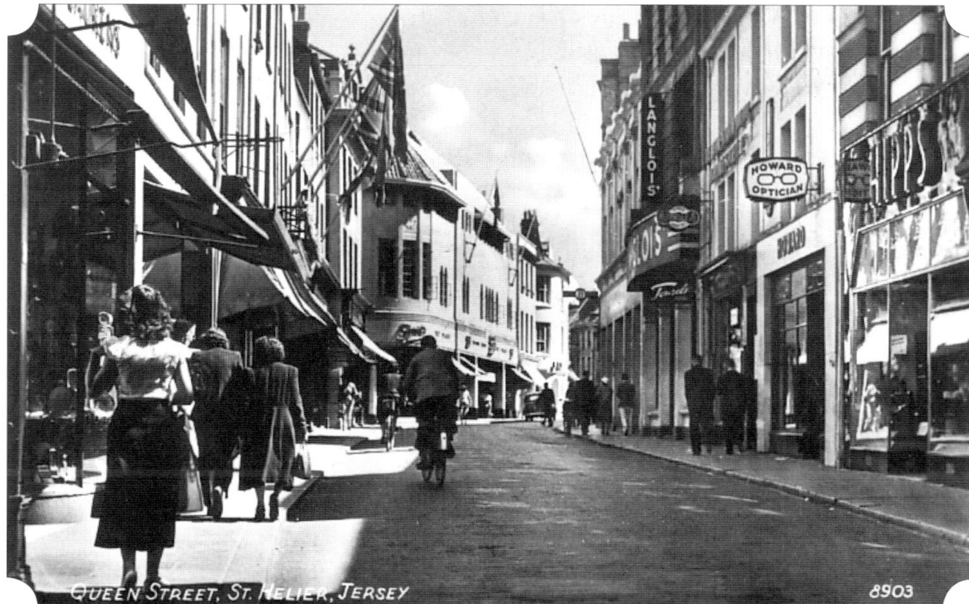

Queen Street. The distinctive façade of the Boots store can be seen in the middle distance. This card was posted on 20th July, 1953. The message is given top opposite with the correspondent expressing reservations about arriving by plane, unlike most holidaymakers new to flying at this time.

'Dear Phyl.
Hope you have nice weather when you go on your holiday. I would like it better if not so many hills. We both took poor view of the plane flight.

Love Gert

~

A message sent to Mr Mandy in Cardiff and postmarked 7 August 1934:

My dear Edwin
"Sunny" Jersey is not living up to its reputation - rain every day so far. Pity the weather's disappointing - it's a marvellous place. Shall be back on Sunday - if not washed away before then.

Au revoir, B

PS Have gained a least 2 stone'

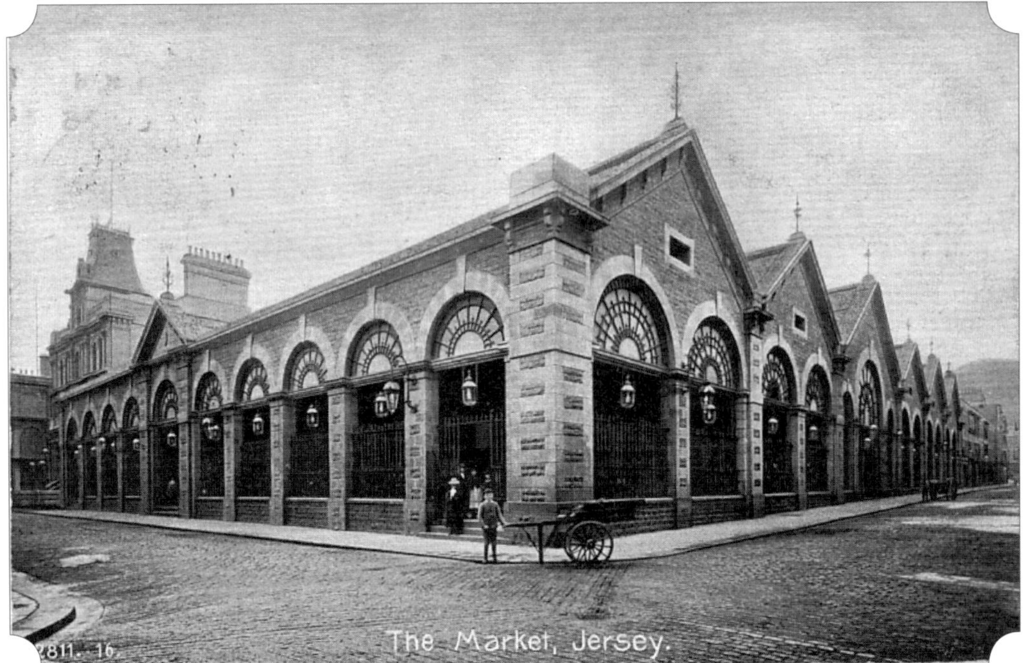

Message to Mrs S of Malmesbury, postmarked 19th June, 1955:

'Having a good time here. Very warm with lots of sunshine. Have been in the sea & in the pubs. Am now like a red indian.

Cheers, Mabel'

The Market, viewed from the junction of Beresford Street and Halkett Place. Opened in 1882 and recently carefully restored, it remains one of the great buildings of St Helier.

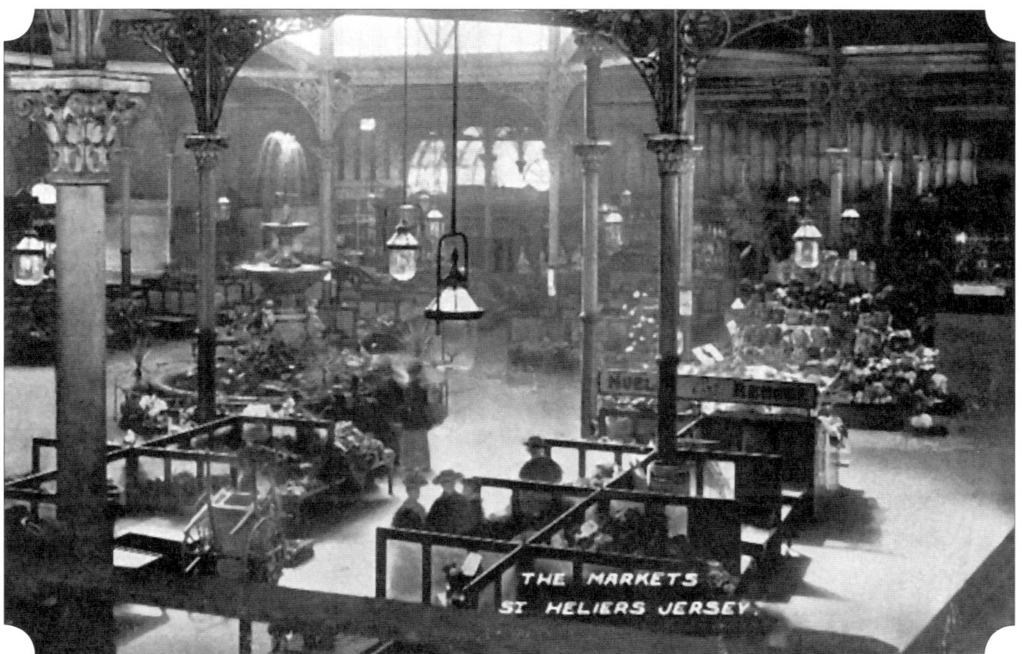

Looking down on market stalls – Huelin Renouf in evidence. Note gas lighting in addition to natural light flooding in through the roof

Message from a disgruntled Gladys to Mrs Cox of Sheffield,

12th July, 1938:

Dear Mum & Dad
Weather here simply terrible - very cold & wet. No sun since Friday. We can't even get English newspapers while the weather is so bad.
Love Gladys'

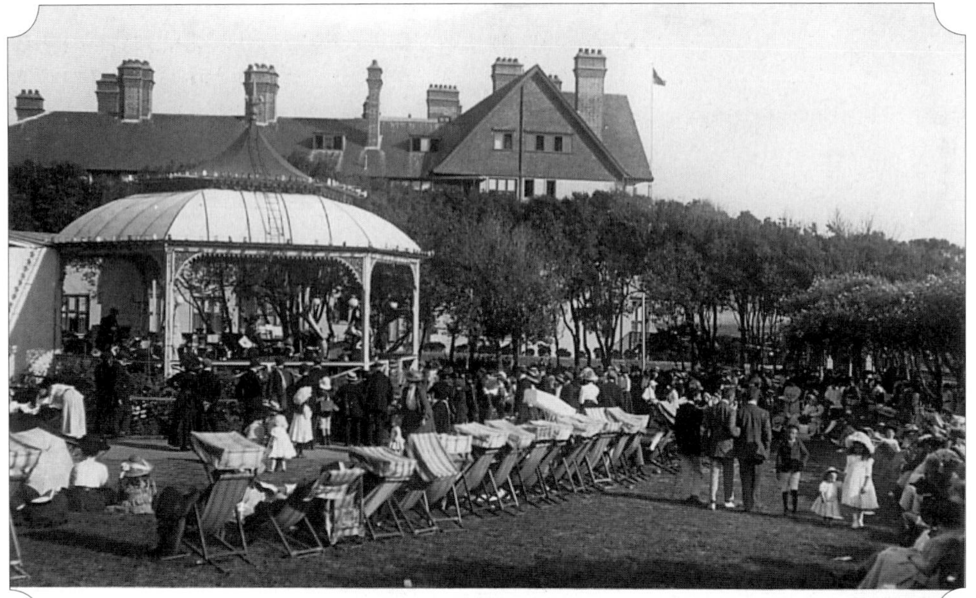

Message from postcard sent to Mr & Mrs Hawlins of Walsall:

'Dear Mother
Just to let you know we arrived safely late on Saturday night after a nightmare journey - never come to Jersey unless by air! The hotel is very good but conditions generally are poor. Food very expensive indeed compared to n/c. Only things cheap are make-up, perfume and high class leather goods. It is a smokers paradise - will bring some back for Dad. Bought a camera today so will have some snaps to show you.

Love Eileen'

Triangle Park. The bandstand stood where the statue of Queen Victoria now stands, it having been moved from the Weighbridge (now Liberation Square). The former name of this open space owes its origin to its shape, wedged as it is between the three boundaries formed by Pierson Road, St Aubins Road and The Esplanade. it is now known as Victoria Park.

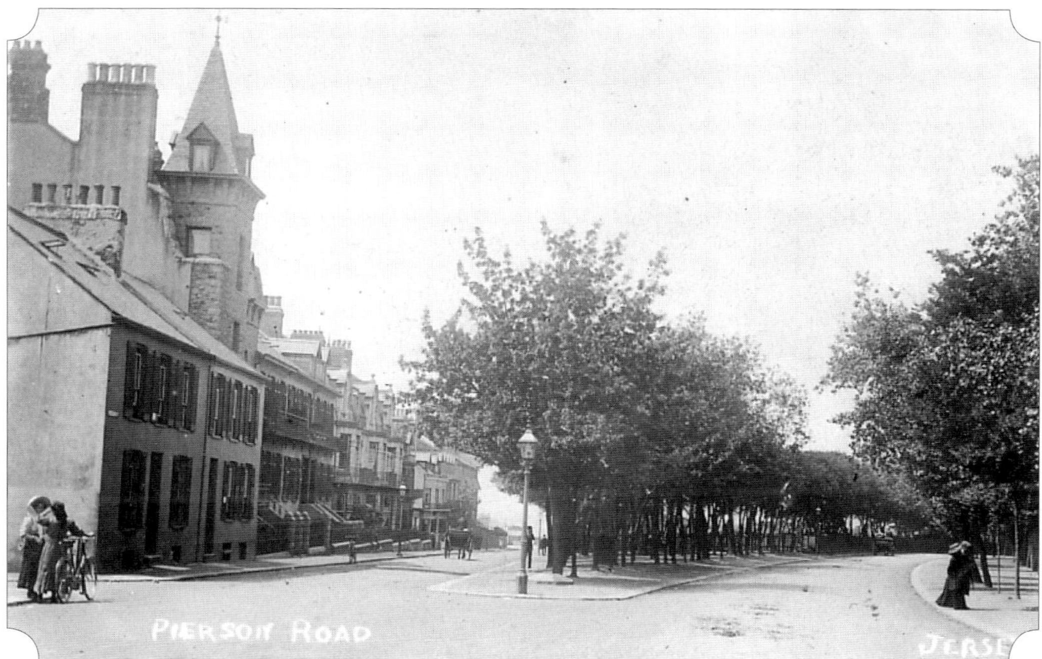

From a postcard sent to Mrs & Miss N of Norwich, 7th August, 1954:

'We are thoroughly enjoying our stay in Jersey. It is very pretty and the various bays so different from each other. the town is so packed with people but it is still possible to get away & find a quiet beach. Today it is very wild & we do wish the weather would become more settled.

WWR'

View along Pierson Road with the apex of Triangle Park in middle foreground. The east side (to the left) consists of a range of attractive Victorian dwellings. The tower once crowned the Cannon Tower Hotel but was removed when it became the Town Park Hotel which closed in 2001. It has since been replaced.

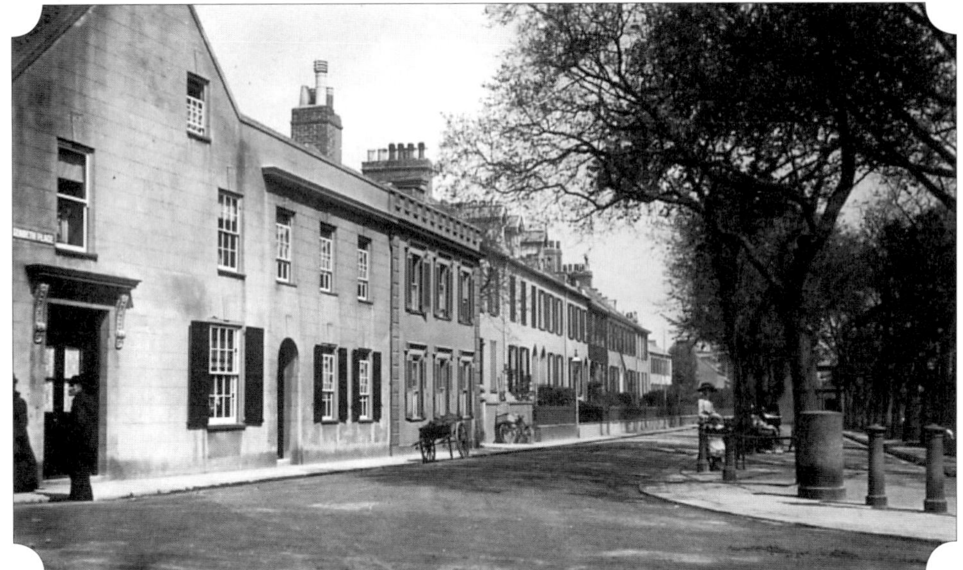

To Mrs Walters of Cardiff in 1910:

'Dear Mother
It is real hot here to-day. I shall have to buy some new white pants. Every one goes in for bathing here although it is not so pleasant for it as the Isle of Wight. The tide goes out very far here.
With love from Alan'

Elizabeth Place. To the right are Parade Gardens whose handsome granite bollards are still intact, if a little the worse for wear. The absence of traffic and parked vehicles certainly allows one to enjoy the perspective.

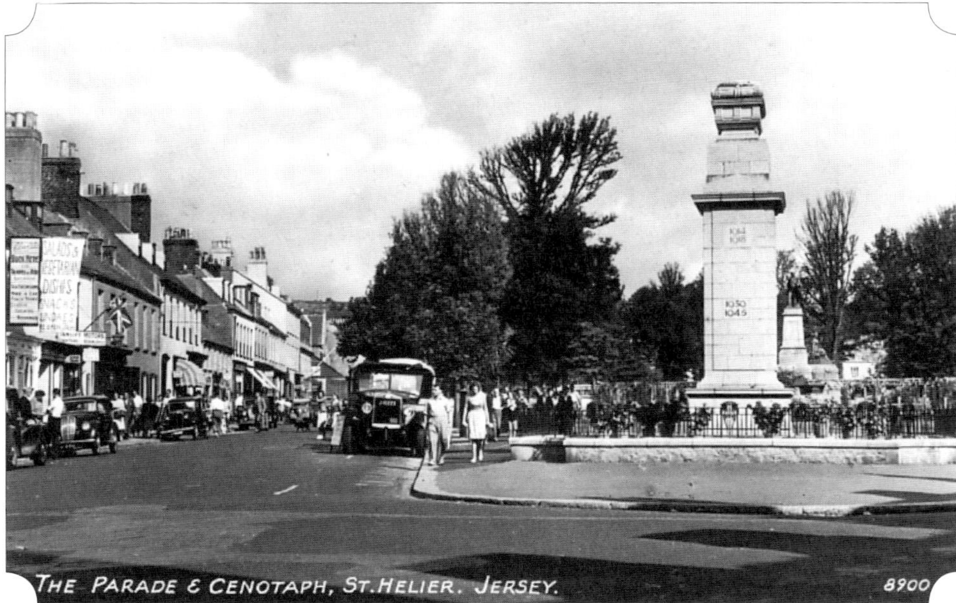

Message to P J Knowles of Kingsteignton, Devon, in 1906:

'Dear Puss
You ought to spend a holiday here to improve your French. The French we spoke (!) before coming was all wrong, but we are quite fluent now.'

Parade Gardens from a different position to the view opposite, probably pictured in the 1950s, featuring the Cenotaph. Tantivy Motors was one of the major businesses running coach tours; their signboard can be seen on the left and a banner advertising 'Salads & Vegetarian Dishes'.

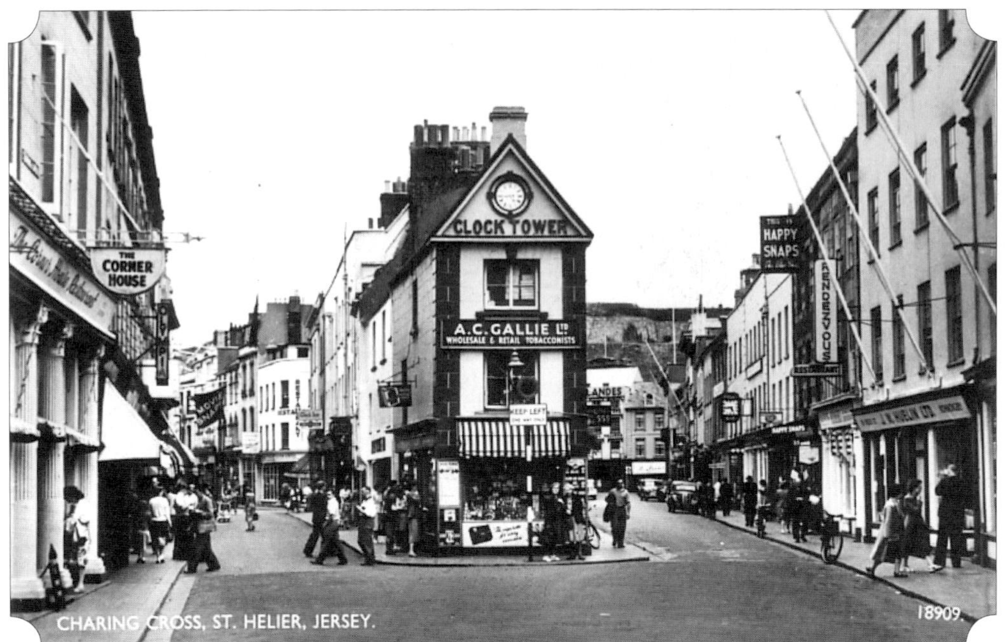

Message sent to Miss W of Exeter, 22nd May, 1953:

'Ommaroo Hotel
We are very happy & comfortable & well-fed here, making plans to cover as much as possible of the Island. I enjoyed the flight very much indeed & could hardly believe what was happening to me.
Yours, M K Stokes'

Today there are many changes of detail in this view of Charing Cross, notably the 1970s' pedestrianisation of King Street, but it is still instantly recognisable.

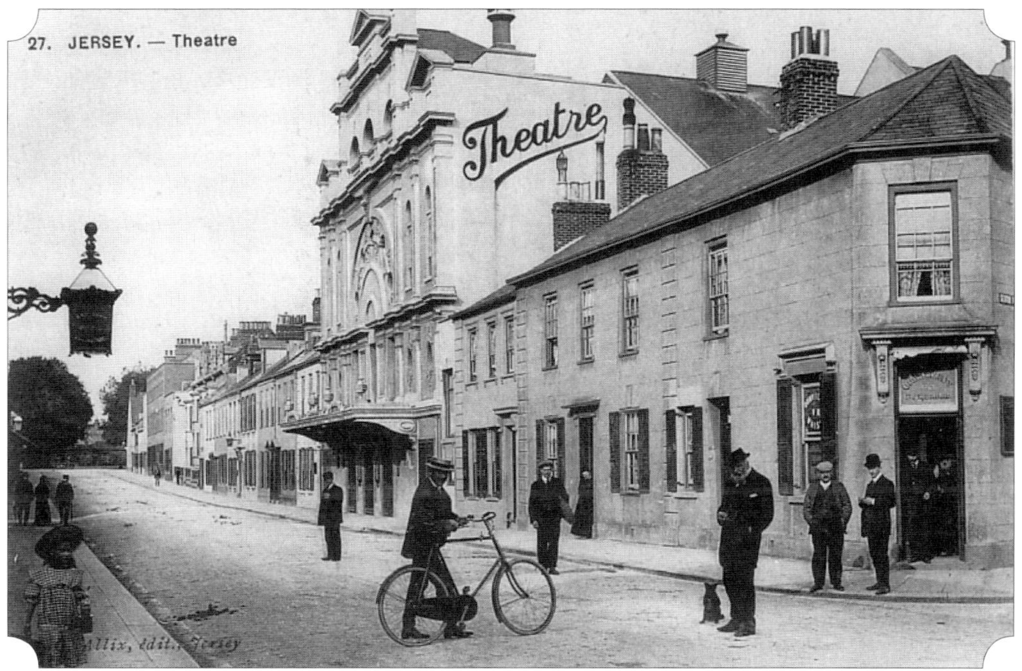

Message sent to Mr & Mrs B of Burnham on Sea, 9th August, 1960:

'We had a lovely journey over, no one was ill, there were over a thousand on board, we arrived at 6. We have good digs, right in the centre of town, it is a bit noisy at night, ever such a large town it has been very hot, getting browned off.
Cheerio, Alf & Ethel'

The Opera House, in Gloucester Street, opened in 1900 by Jerseywoman and internationally famous actress, Lillie Langtry. This landmark building was completely restored and reopened for its centenary year in 2000.

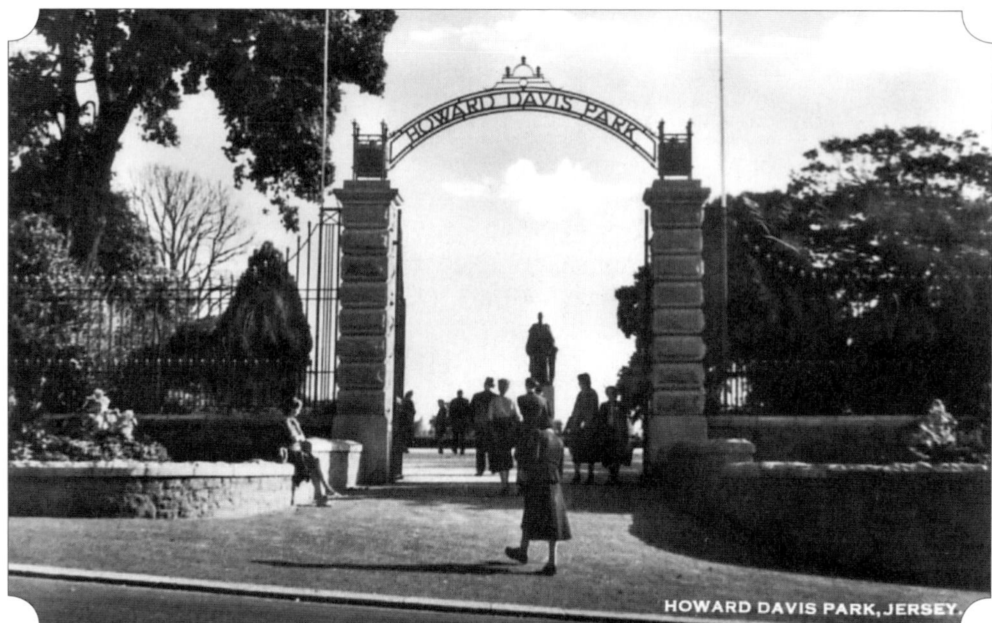

From a booklet on Jersey published by the Jersey Chamber of Commerce in 1955:

'A delightful retreat is found in Howard Davis Park. These beautifully kept grounds, with their trim lawns and well-stocked flower beds, lie on the outskirts of the town of St Helier. Band Concerts and other entertainments are held in the Park during the Summer Season.'

Howard Davis Park was one of many gifts to the island by T.B. Davis, a Jerseyman who made a fortune in shipping in South Africa, in memory of his son Howard who was killed in the First World War.

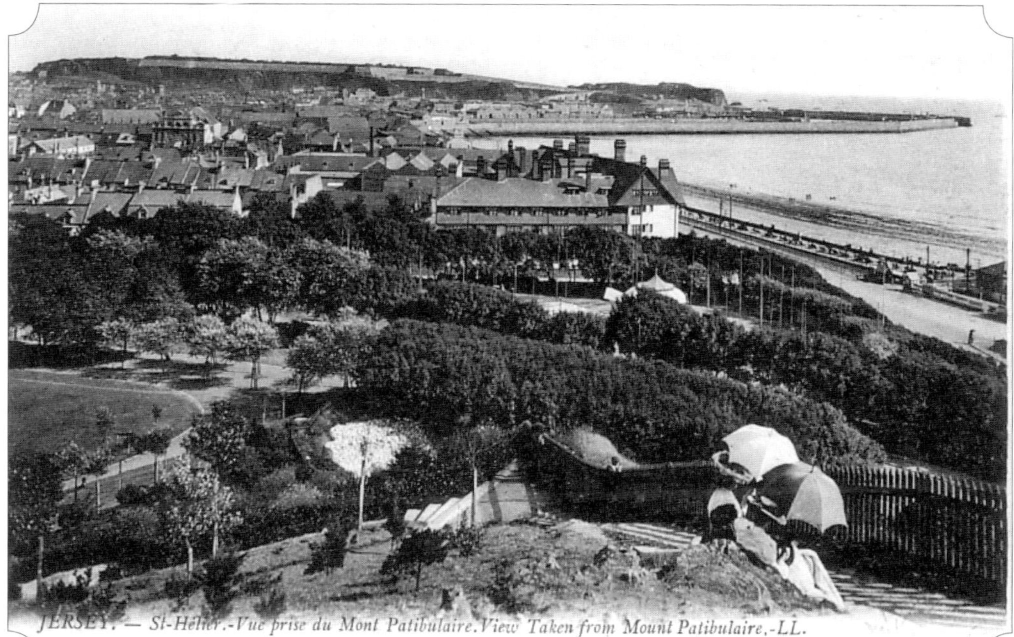

Message from a card postmarked 27th June, 1956, addressed to Miss Pascoe of Bideford, Devon:

'We certainly are lucky with the weather. Wilson says he's only coming back to earn enough money to come to Jersey again. It's an ideal spot. Went to a French revue Monday evening which was very good indeed. See you Friday when we come to earth with a bang.

Love W & Y'

View taken from Mont Patibulaire (otherwise known as West Mount), looking towards the Esplanade at West Park. The most prominent building, apart from the Grand Hotel, is the Opera House and, on the horizon, the granite bastion of Fort Regent.

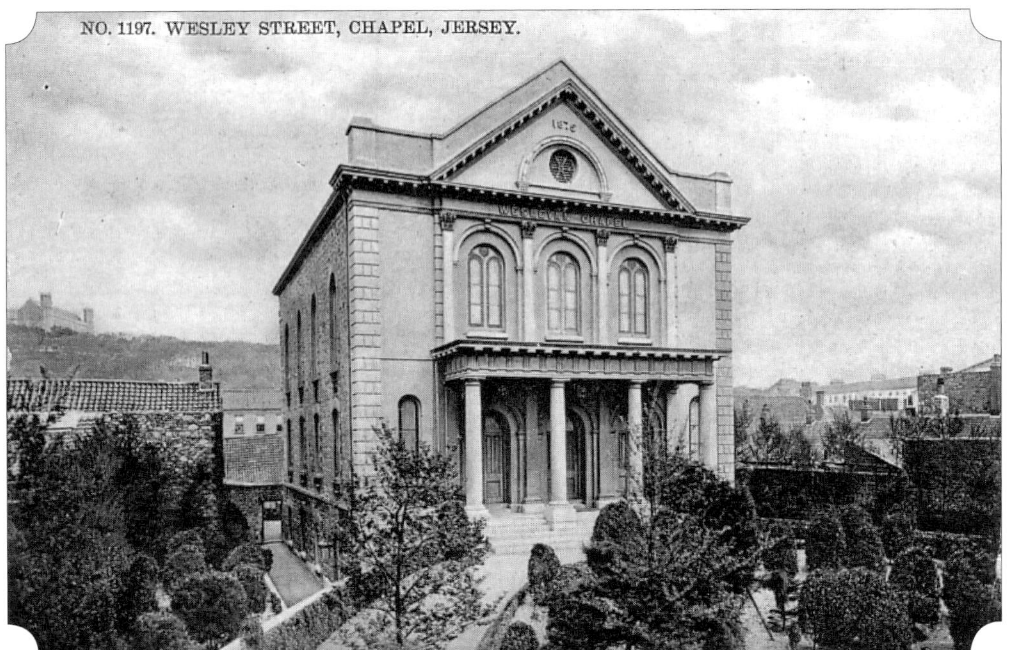

Message on postcard sent in 1948, a time of strict rationing on the mainland:

'The Grand
Spending 14 days here. A very fine Island for a holiday. Lots of stock in shops at reasonable prices. No tax. Want of coupons keeps purchases down to minimum.'

One of many impressively constructed Methodist Chapels in Jersey, several of which are no longer in use as such or have been demolished. The Wesley Street Chapel has recently been heightened and widened in the process of conversion into apartments.

~ St Helier-by-sea ~

One of the features which holidaymakers looked for in a coastal resort was the opportunity for casual strolling along the front, in the vicinity of the beach and sea. St Helier offered this in abundance. On the west side of town is The Esplanade, where folk could wander from the Weighbridge to West Park and beyond. And they could venture over the causeway to Elizabeth Castle – more of an adventure before the reclamation of the beach west of West Pier.

Old guide books extol the attractions of 'West End Bathing Pool', or 'Victoria Marine Lake', as it was sometimes referred to. This opened in 1897: 'There is every convenience for both swimmers and non-swimmers – rafts, spring boards and double diving stage (5 feet and 9 feet high). A boatman is always in attendance.'

The Esplanade was a great place to take the air but 'unfortunately, so severe are the south-west gales during winter that it has proved impossible to get young trees to withstand their devastating effects, and the promenade has consequently a rather bare appearance.'

Most nineteenth century expansion of St Helier took place in a northerly direction; the St Luke's area on the far side of Fort Regent was not fully developed until the first quarter of the twentieth century, although the shoreline at Havre des Pas had been an important area for shipbuilding in the 1800s.

As the tourism industry developed, more hotels and boarding houses opened in this area and the promenade at La Collette, with its incomparable gardens, were created.

The present reclamation of the foreshore at La Collette will change forever the aspect for promenaders here but there remains the enjoyable stroll along the front past the slipway by the former Hotel de la Plage and the dramatically curved sea wall before reaching the Bathing Pool at Havre des Pas (opened in 1895) and on to the Dicq.

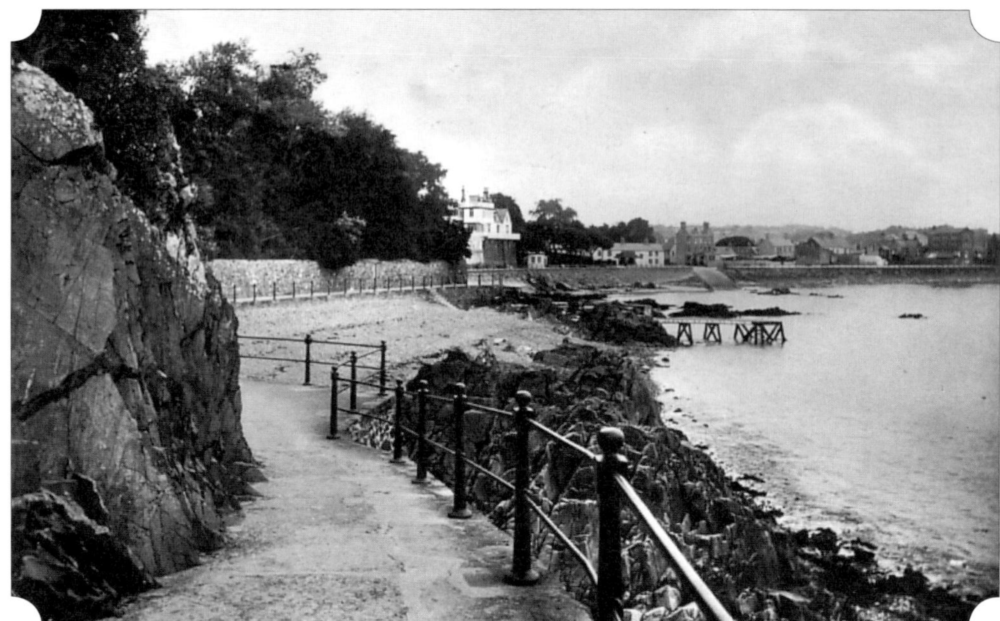

View eastwards along La Collette featuring the diving stage of the Jersey Swimming Club. The card is postmarked 23rd August, 1932.

~

Message on postcard sent to Miss C of Bath, 22nd August, 1959:

'Weather still grand. Thunderstorm from 10.30pm through the night. No other rain at all. Overcast this morning. Just going to the park. A ride yesterday afternoon. Good TV reception here. Think Mrs S cat run over this morning. 3 more in today. 7 altogether now.

Love Doll'

A guide book from 1937: 'From the south end of Pier Road a path winds round the stunted tower called La Collette, near which is the Men's Bathing Station (free). At high tide the bathers enter the water from a wooden pier; at low water from specially prepared diving places among the rocks, to which access is gained by cement paths.'

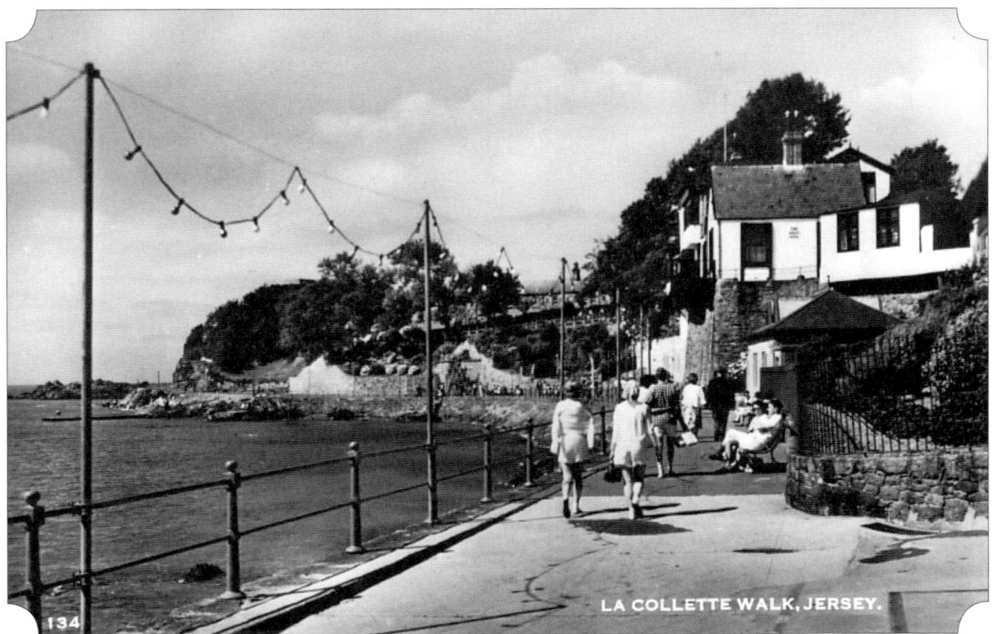

A sunny view westwards taken from near the slipway which is the meeting point of La Collette and Havre des Pas.

Message to Miss Joan Slade of Orpington:

'Dear Joan,
I am enjoying myself very much here but my parents don't like the 'atmosphere' much. I won the mixed doubles table tennis last week. I'll be bringing some photos taken at dances.

Jeff'

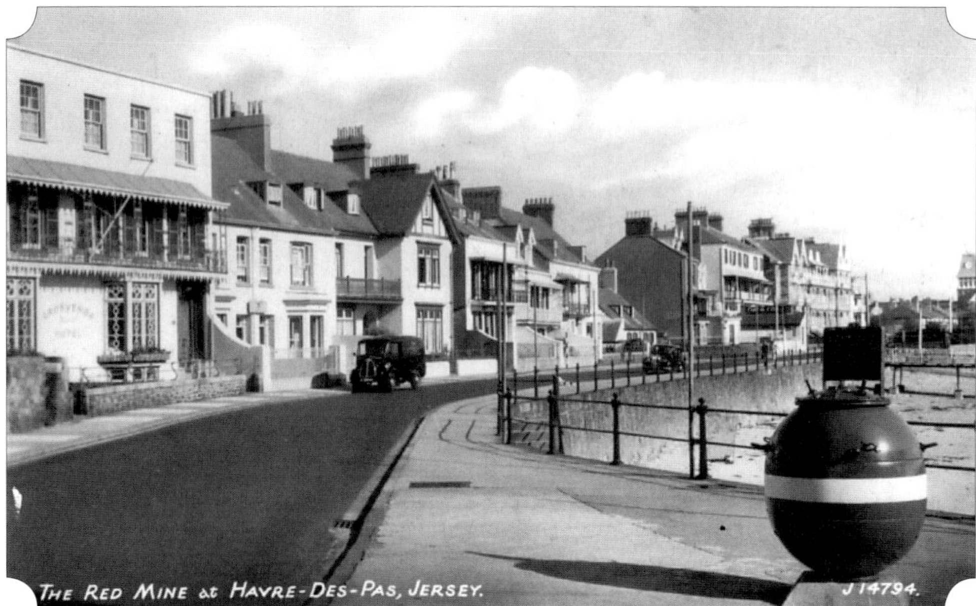

Message written in 1946:

'Dear All
You would all love a holiday here if you come by air as I did. It was a glorious trip of 1 hr 40 mins from Croydon. Jersey is very nice & the little bays all round the island are really beautiful & quiet. The weather has been simply glorious & we are enjoying every moment of our stay here. Milk is not rationed & wherever you go you see people buying glasses of milk just as you do ice cream. In the hotel at lunch times it is strange to see grown up people all ordering glasses of milk with their lunch. Hotel is also licensed.

Fred'

A guide book from 1937: 'A promenade, substantiially built of granite and cement, with seats every few yards, leads from La Collette to the Havre des Pas Esplanade, and at its eastern end passes several cafés. some in the open air – a little group that reminds one very strongly of Continental resorts, especially in the evening.'

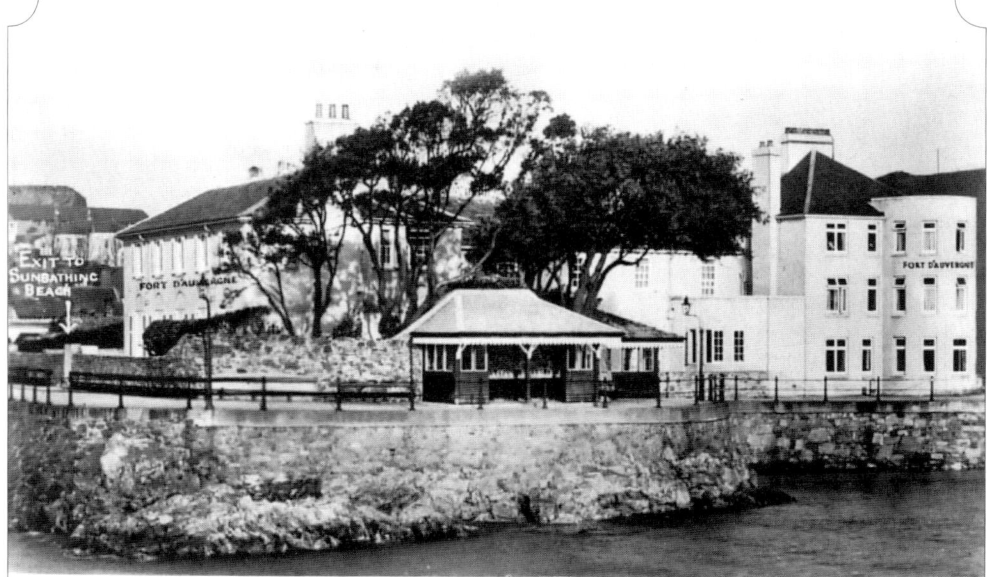

Fort d'Auvergne Hotel, Havre-Des-Pas, Jersey

This card is postmarked 29th July 1954 and bears the following message:

My Dear Susan,
Thought you might like this picture of our Hotel here, the window fourth from the left as you look at the card is our bedroom. No rain this week, but such a terrible high wind it nearly blows us away. Looking forward to the Battle of Flowers. See you soon. Love to all.
Auntie & Uncle.

Fort D'Auvergne Hotel, Havre des Pas. Note the lettering and arrow on left-hand side ondicating 'Exit to Sunbathing Beach' which probably means this customised view was specially commissioned by the Hotel.

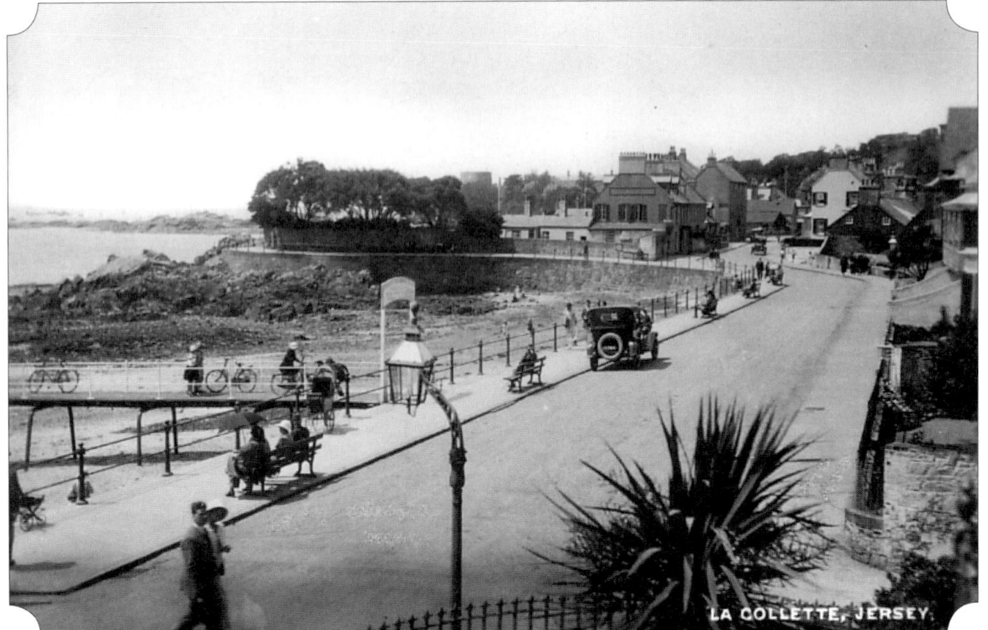

Captioned 'La Collette', but more accurately Havre des Pas, looking east from the junction with Roseville Street. The former footbrdige to the Bathing Pool is on the left and has been replaced latterly. This card most likely dates from the 1920s.

A visitor from Guernsey in 1934 wrote home:

'We had a most glorious crossing & Mum wasn't ill at all. The traffic here is awful, much worse than Guernsey.'

~

Message to Mrs J of Erdington, Birmingham, in 1957:

'Having rather nice weather at present with plenty to eat and being waited on at the hotel by French waiters.
From Mrs Green'

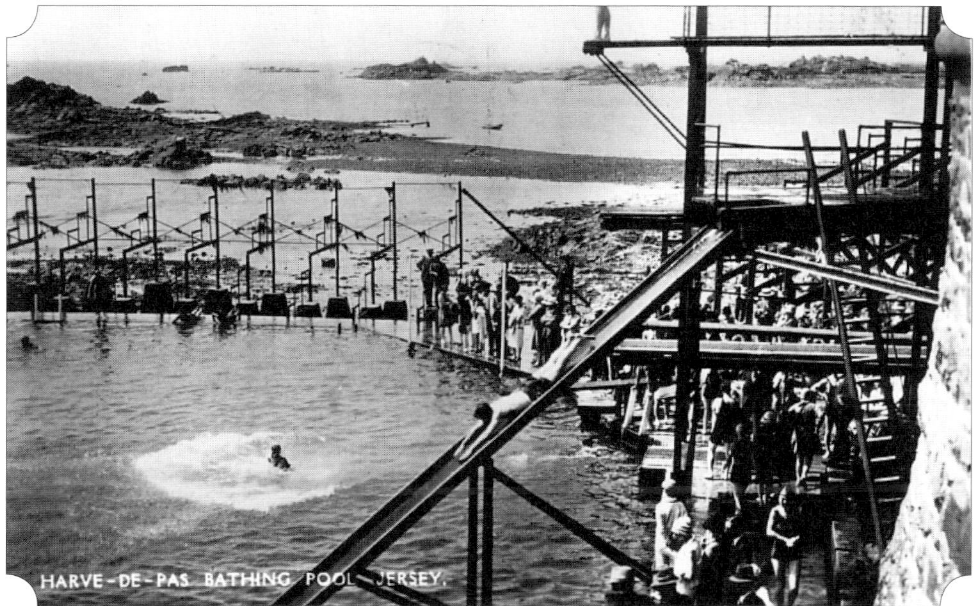

The fun people had before Health and Safety rules and regulations put an end to diving boards! Probably 1930s.

A guide book of 1937: 'The pool is roughly horse-shoe shaped: its wall encloses an area of over 2 acres. At the shallow end is a special place for beginners and non-swimmers. The depth increases to 12 feet under the high diving stage. Spring boards and fixed boards are provided for divers. There are swimming courses of 110 and 50 yeards, over which a national championship is generally held once a year. In addition, various swimming galas take place. One of the most exciting events is the annual swimming match between Jersey and Guernsey when some excellent racing is seen, as the two islands are very keen rivals. Overlooking the shallow end of the pool is a terrace where sun-bathing can be enjoyed at leisure and where refreshments may be obtained. On Tuesday and Friday evenings this terrace is the scene of open-air dancing.'

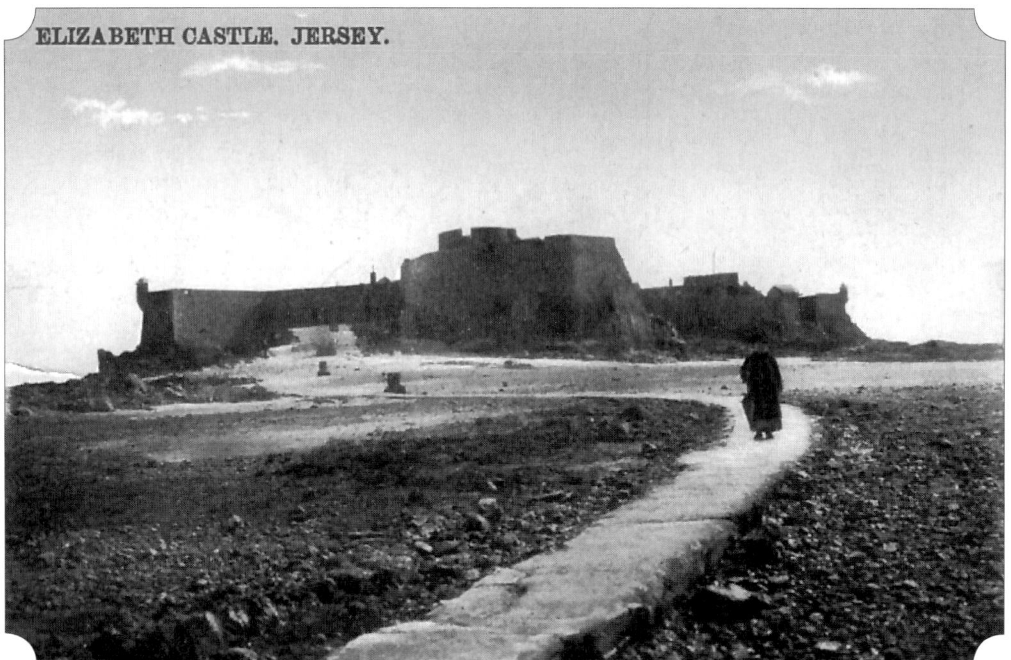

Message sent in 1949:

'We have had a most perfect week, but a week does not really warrant the journey. We have completely toured the coast of the island. Everything brown instead of green under the very hot sun and nearly all the inhabitants speaking French (a patois thereof) amongst themselves.'

A solitary figure returning along the causeway from Elizabeth Castle at low tide, a trek which thousands of Jersey vistors have made.

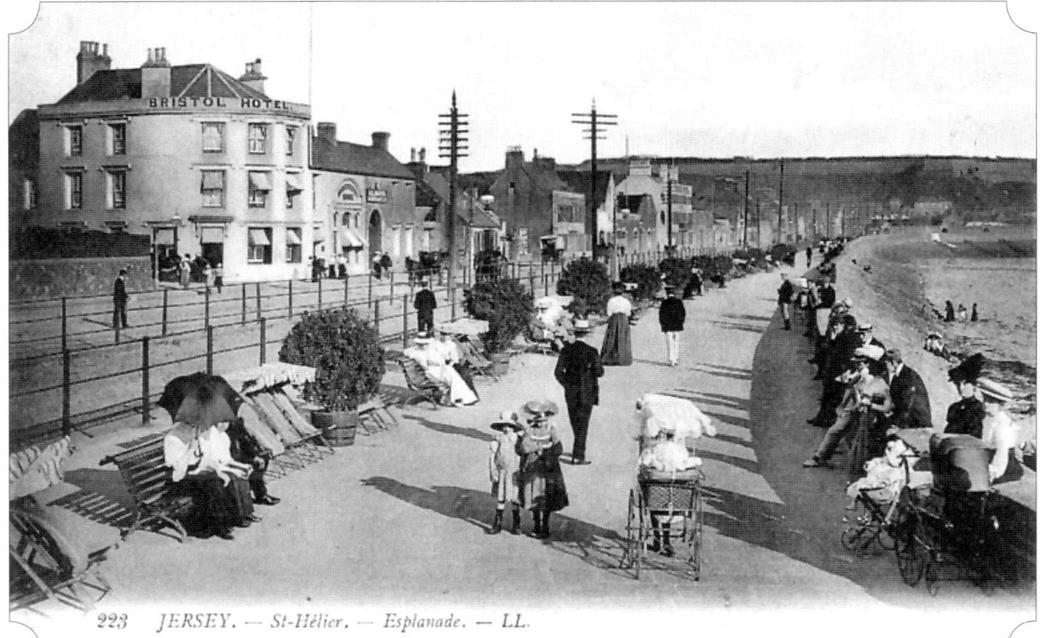

To Mr Brown of Winchester:

'We apparently do not know what sunshine, surf & also rain are in England. Here everything is on an enlarged scale. We are having a truly great time. Had to shelter on the hill here from a waterspout. Some fine Janes here.'

View east along the promenade at West Park. Note the Bristol Hotel on the corrner of Kensington Place which, at the time of writing, awaits redevelopment. See also the railed enclosure for the railway track and the absence of high-rise buildings along the Esplanade.

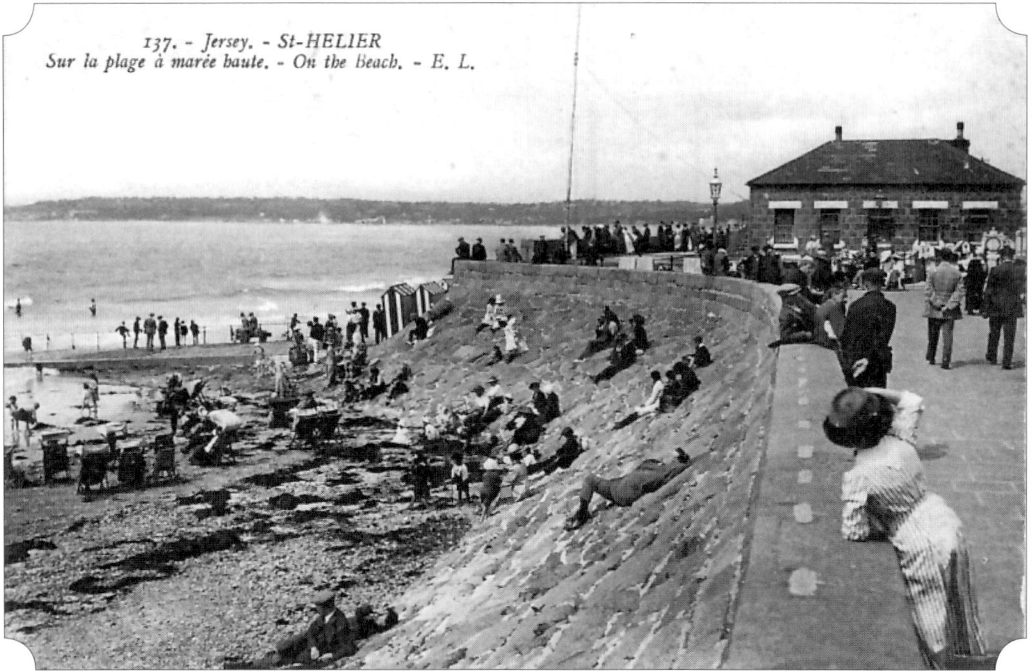

Message from 1929:

'Here are the three lost souls gazing at the mud or sea having passed this Castle on a 2/6 tour. We had a fairly good crossing. The hotel is quite nice: the weather lovely: so all is well.'

Looking west along the promenade at West Park. Note the stripy bathing huts, which bathers used for changing, on the slipway and the railing along its right-had side. The single-storey building on the right was a military picket house, used when a detachment of soldiers was stationed at Elizabeth Castle.

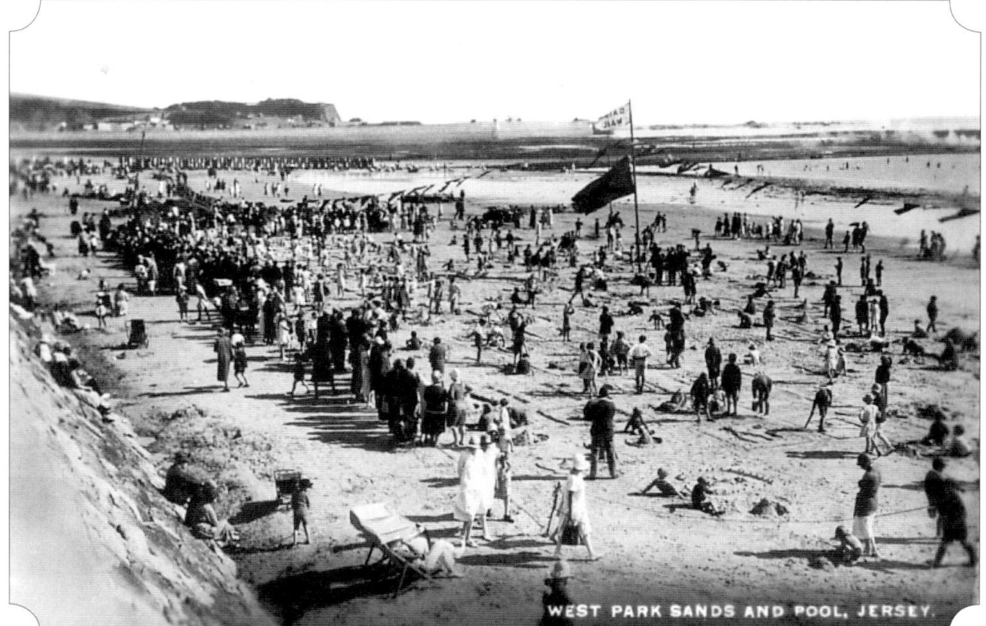

Looking down along the beach at West Park, most likely between the wars. The flag near the centre denotes the Daily Mail Sand Castle Building Competition, the sort of organised fun which would be unusual today.

Addressed to Miss Collins of Teignmouth, Devon, postmarked 25th August, 1932, its message reads:

'This is a marvellous place - weather brilliant but not too overpowering. Hotel seems fairly normal tho' some of the people rather mad. Food good tell your mother. Have done a trip to Greve de Lecq and one round the island - marvellous bathing beaches. Two rather nice fellows here, met them out at sea - went to West Park Pavilion with them.

Love Hilda'

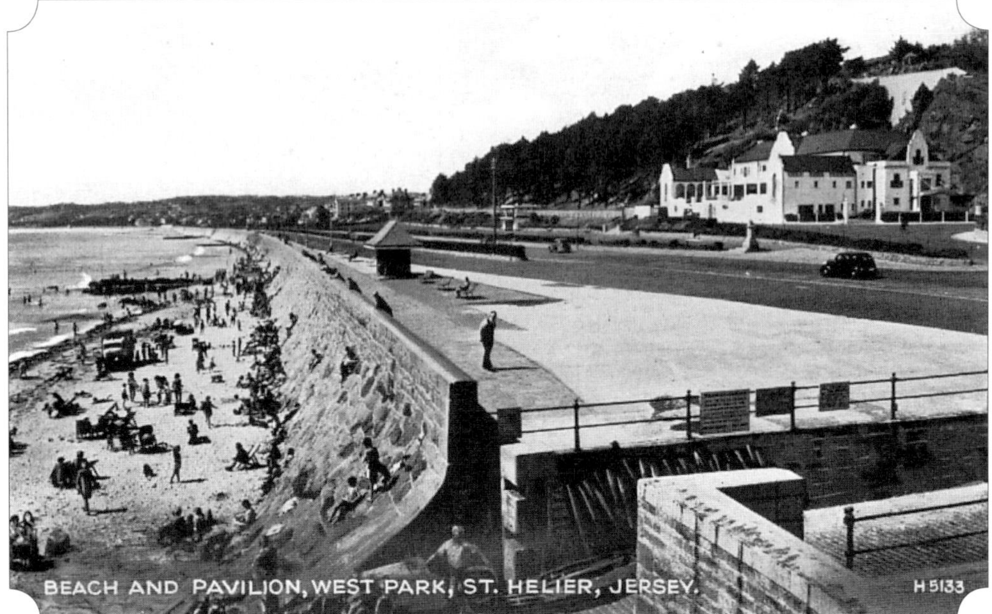
BEACH AND PAVILION, WEST PARK, ST. HELIER, JERSEY. H 5133

A message to a chum in 1958:

'Dear Nobby
Having a very nice time here with bags of talent about but most of it's sixteen or sixty. They've got scooters here but they keep braking [sic] down. Having a good old session every night & what with that and swimming every day I feel just about clapped out.

Brian'

Looking west from West Park. the entrance to the slipway to the beach visible here has disappeared, access to the beach now being provided by a flight of steps. The distinctive Pavilion, built in 1931, can be seen below the eminence of West Mount.

~ Trip around the Island ~

A small island with such varied scenery demanded to be seen, and the means of doing so has developed over the years of tourism in Jersey.

A hundred years ago, visitors toured in horse-drawn carriages, known as excursion cars: 'During the summer, excursion cars leave St Helier several times daily for all parts of the Island, and are largely patronised. Each car has a conductor who points out objects of interest, en route, and endeavours to be of use to everybody, even to the extent of obliging with songs and music.'

Two prominent livery stables were Down's in David Place and the Paragon in Grove Place. Horse-drawn excursion cars were followed in the 1920s by motor charabancs, then by motor coaches: 'During the summer it is possible to visit almost every beauty spot in the island by motor-coach. The majority of these vehicles start from the open space at the Weighbridge. There are daily trips around the Island, leaving between 10 and 11am and returning in time for dinner, while shorter afternoon and evening trips specialize in particular localities. The fares are usually about 5s. for a day trip, 2s.6d afternoon, and 2s. evening.' This advice was published in a guide book in 1937. The prices remained much the same throughout the 1950s.

There were always alternatives to the organised coach tour – Edwardian visitors loved to walk, often availing themselves of the train to reach starting points or to return to town. Many visitors brought their bicycles with them or hired machines once in the island. And latterly, of course, many visitors hire cars to get around the Island.

The postcard views that follow are arranged in an anti-clockwise direction, which is how I remember the Round the Island coach tour in the 1950s.

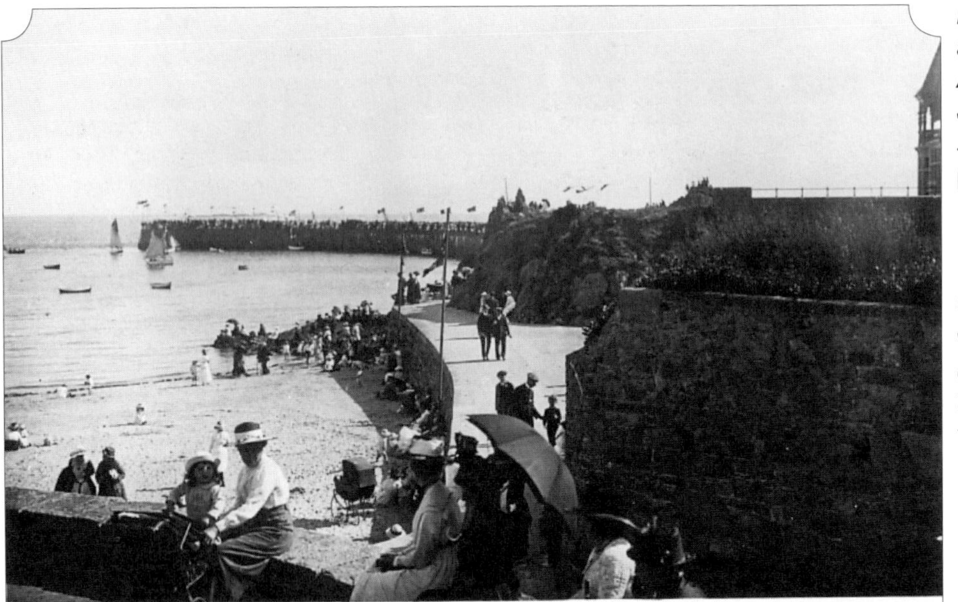

PITT SERIES No. 87 LA ROCQUE HARBOUR (REGATTA DAY), JERSEY PHOTO F. FOOT

Message sent in 1935 to an addressee in Perth, Western Australia:

'I had a lovely picnic given me at this place "La Rocque" Jersey. The beaches are beautiful.'

~

Message sent in 1951:

'This is an ideal place for a holiday. Continual sunshine, lovely beaches, 1st class Hotel and French cooking - we must all come here.'

The Gorey Regatta, founded in 1857, is one of the world's oldest. It is open to visitng and local sailors and is held along the island's east coast. Here we see spectators gathering at La Rocque Harbour to view the day's events.

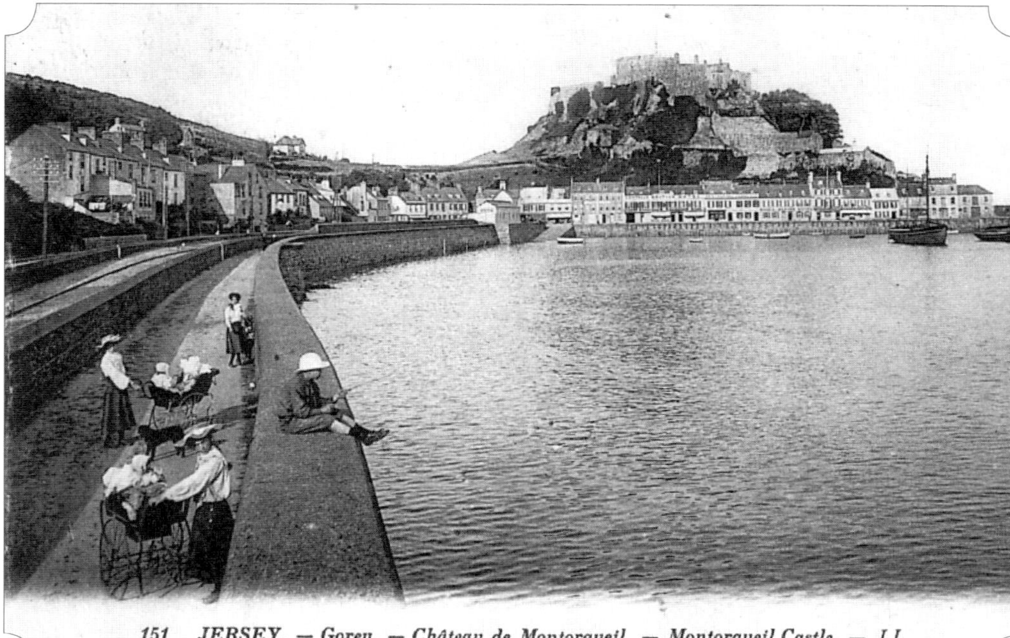

151 JERSEY. — Gorey. — Château de Montorgueil. — Montorgueil Castle. — LL

View from the sea wall at high tide. The promenade is well protected from both the sea and the railway track.

Message on postcard sent in 1929:

Dear Eva
Here are the three lost souls gazing at the mud or sea having just passed this Castle on a 2/6 tour. We had a fairly good crossing. The hotal is quite nice; the weather lovely: so all is well. Best love to your big daughter and the rest of the noisy crowd.
Love Ida, Annie and Gertie

~

To Miss C Barry of Lyme Regis, Dorset, 25th July, 1931:

'I hope your spots have gone and that you are feeling quite OK. I walked seven miles to see this Castle! The weather is glorious but my arms are blistered with the sun.
Love from Nurse

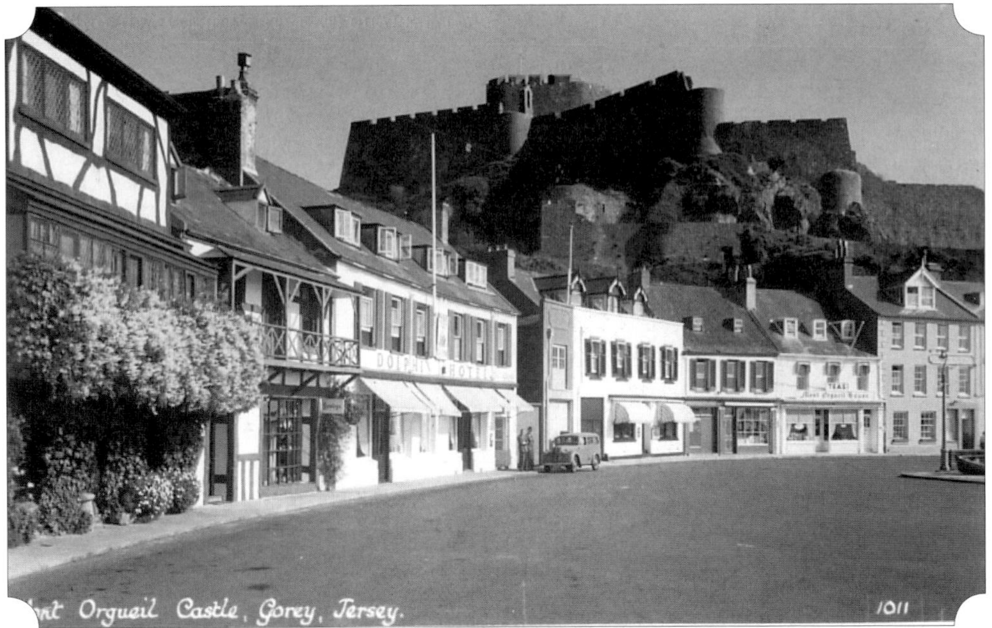

A nicely composed picture of the attractive sweep of buildings lining Gorey Pier with the shapely bulk of Mont Orgueil Castle looming beyond.

Message sent to addressee in Rochdale in 1926:

' Jersey is a wonderful place - everything is of such a vivid colour, rocks, seas, sky and vegetation is like none I have ever seen - everything seems huge conpared to things at home.'

~

From 1951:

'Still enjoying life here. All looking like niggers. Feel I could stay another week, but all good things come to an end.'

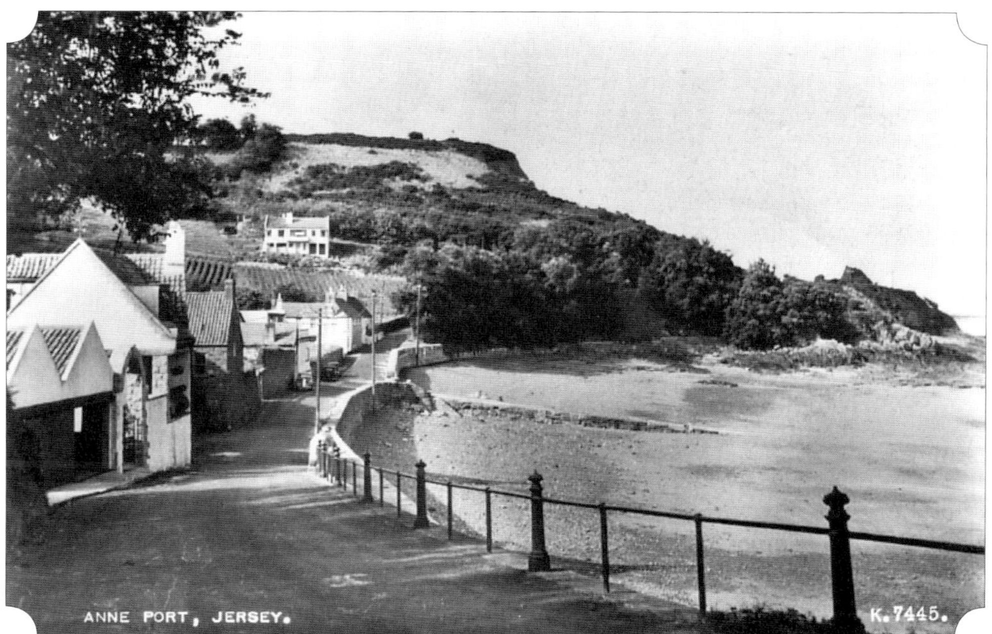

Anne Port, a pretty east coast bay as uncommercialised now as it was when this picture was taken, perhaps in the 1950s.

Message sent in 1954:

'Having a very happy time. Weather just to our liking. Both enjoyed plane journey & have finished coming by sea as saving of time makes such a difference. We are both feeling very refreshed and well. This time next week back to usual routine. We leave Thurs 3.15. I think one pint of milk & a small loaf will do.'

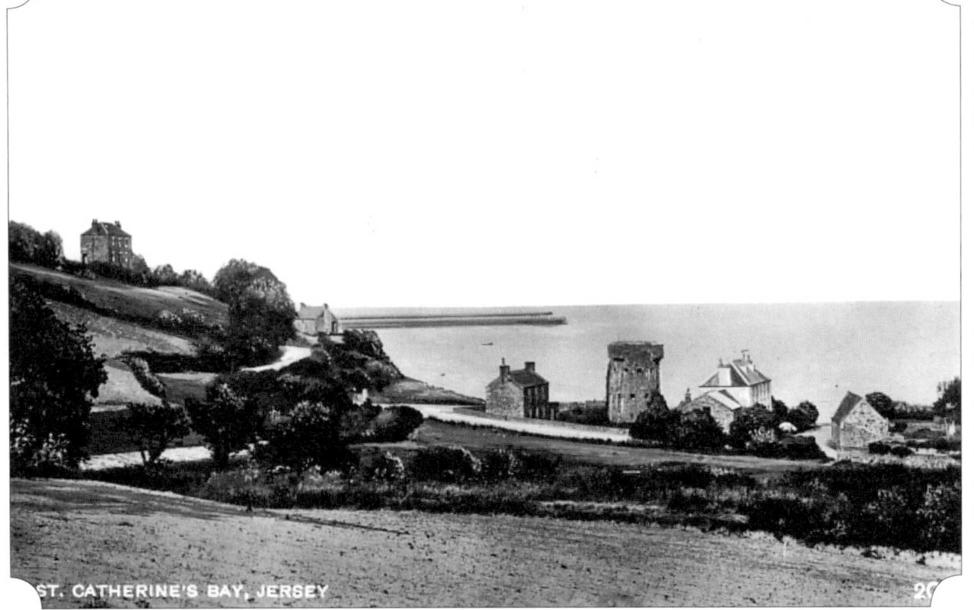

View to St Catherine's Bay with the breakwater in the distance and the Martello Tower at La Mare closer to hand.

Message from 1946:

'Had a lovely day on a farm yesterday, plenty to eat, the bread and cakes are much nicer than ours.

Love Lillian'

~

Message sent in 1954:

'Dear All
Having a grand time. Weather is excellent. The Hotel is very good with plenty to eat. Drinks & cigs are cheap, so we are making the most of it. Flying to Guernsey next week for a day.

Ray & Molly'

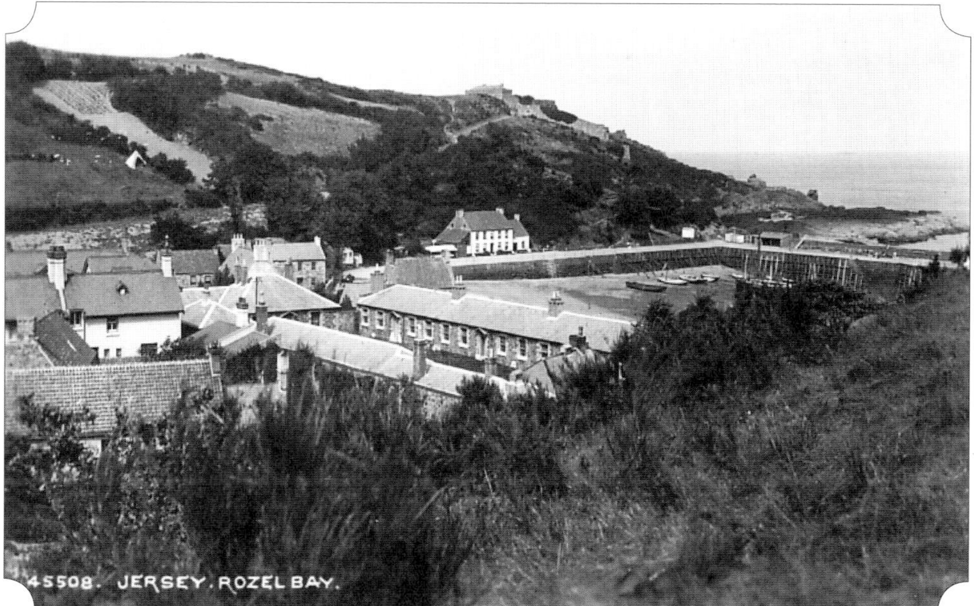

Rozel Bay. An early twentieth century view with Rozel barracks, built about 1910, in the foreground. The message on this card is reproduced on the right.

Message sent in 1922:

'The White House, Rozel Bay

Hello, old top! How are you? I thought you might like a glimpse of Rozel so I am sending you this with an abundance of love. Cheerio! I shall be home on the 24th so look out for a good time coming! We are having a gorgeous time here this next week, and last week we were booked up every day. I will tell you all about it when I come. Tomorrow we are anticipating a sail around the island. I am longing to see Mother and Daddie and you all again, but quite tearful at the thought of leaving this darling little isle and all my friends here.

My very best love to you and all.
Yours ever, Margo'

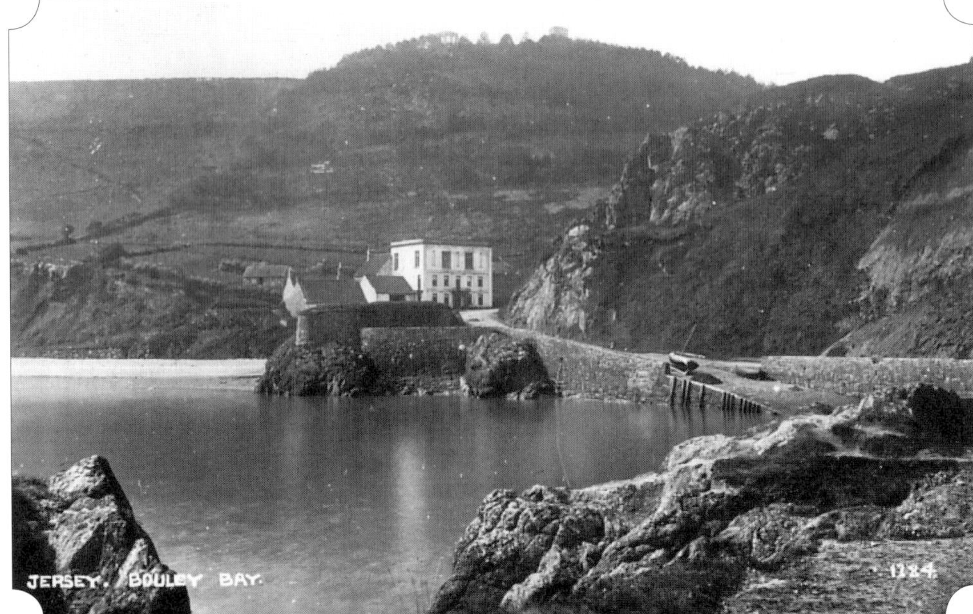

A calm and uncrowded view of the Bouley Bay Hotel from the pier.
Even if they did not descend as far as the beach, a view across the bay from the high ground of Jardin d'Olivet was a must for early tourists.

Message sent to Mr J Nowell of Balham, London, in 1950:

Dear Jeffery
Here is a pleasant view of one of the bays. I've toured most of the Island by cycle, using a map of pubs! The French wines are extremely palatable.
See you soon, Sid'

~

To Mr P Gomes of Kingston on Thames, Surrey, sent 20th June, 1927:

'My dear Phil
How are things going? Alright I hope: Saturday night was the time of our lives. I was glad to see daylight. Everything is quite nice now. Marie & Fred have gone a trip today. The cars come to the door & gather the people, fine isn't it! So is the weather.
Love Mum'

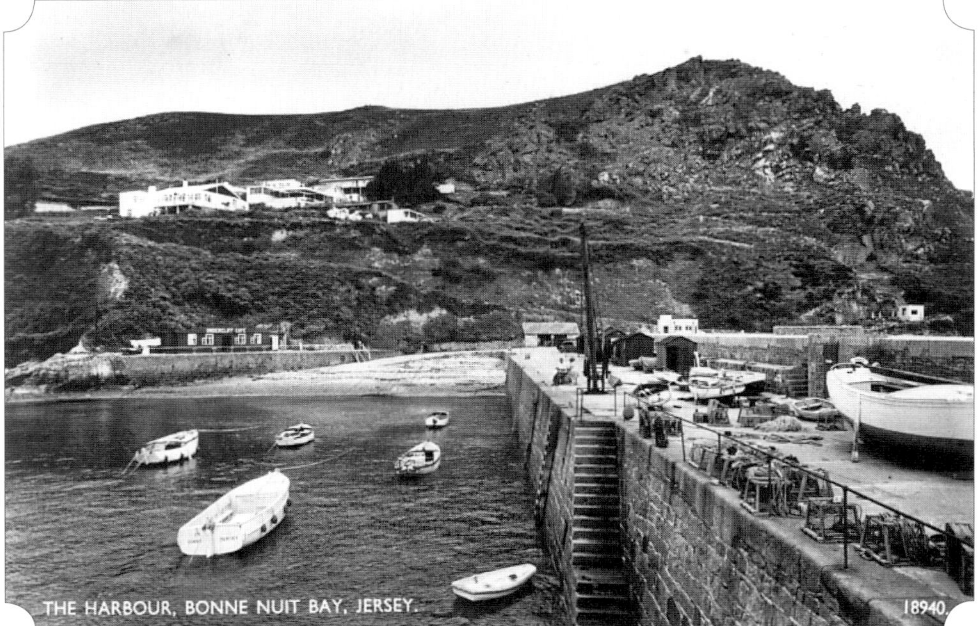

Message on postcard sent 30th September, 1953:

'This is a small island but it is full of good spots. Today we went exploring the North Coast, with grand rocky cliffs and headlands and jolly little sandy coves. And what sand - acres & acres of it in some places - more than Richard could possibly fill with railways. Weather fine some days but always warm. A good time is being had by all. You would like the warm airs.

Love J'

According to a nineteenth century guide book: 'The descent to Bonne Nuit from the picturesque quarries of Mont Mado is very beautiful, and includes a rich variety of rock and water scenery, with reefs of rock running out into sea at a short distance.'

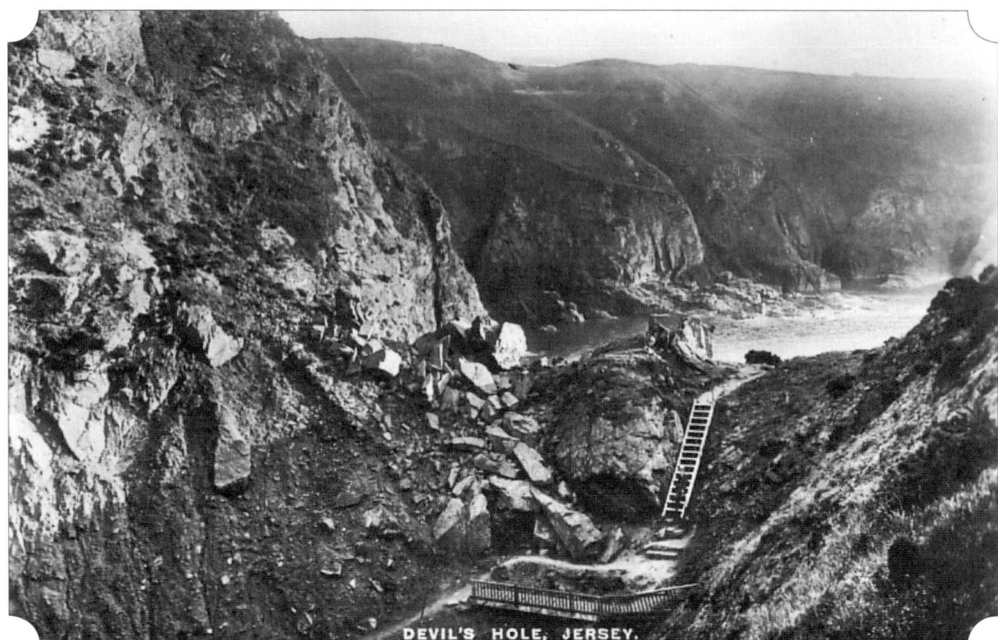

From a guide book, 1921: 'Rounding a dome-shaped hill, we reach a small refreshment bar. Here twopence is paid for the right of descent, much easier than in the case of the Wolf's Cave, and visitors can also see a caged black figure, with horns and tail, flap his wings and nod his head when a rope is pulled from the inside. Many visiting cards are left for his Satanic Majesty.'

Message from a postcard sent 13th July, 1927, to Mr Counsell of Cardiff:

'2 Edward Place, Royal Parade
St Helier, Jersey, C.I.

Dear Ed,
Having a real good time here. We visited Devil's Hole yesterday and also met him. It's very cold down there, but jolly hot climbing back. Took a snap of it, so hope it is a success. I can tell you we are getting quite experts at climbing. Had to climb 500ft to see Wolfs Caves before we visited Devil's Hole. Then we went on to Greve de Lecq where there is a beautiful stretch of sands but we were swarmed and some kiddies from a creche who wanted to turn my bag inside out, but we moved on - nothing doing. the drive through country was glorious.

Agnes'

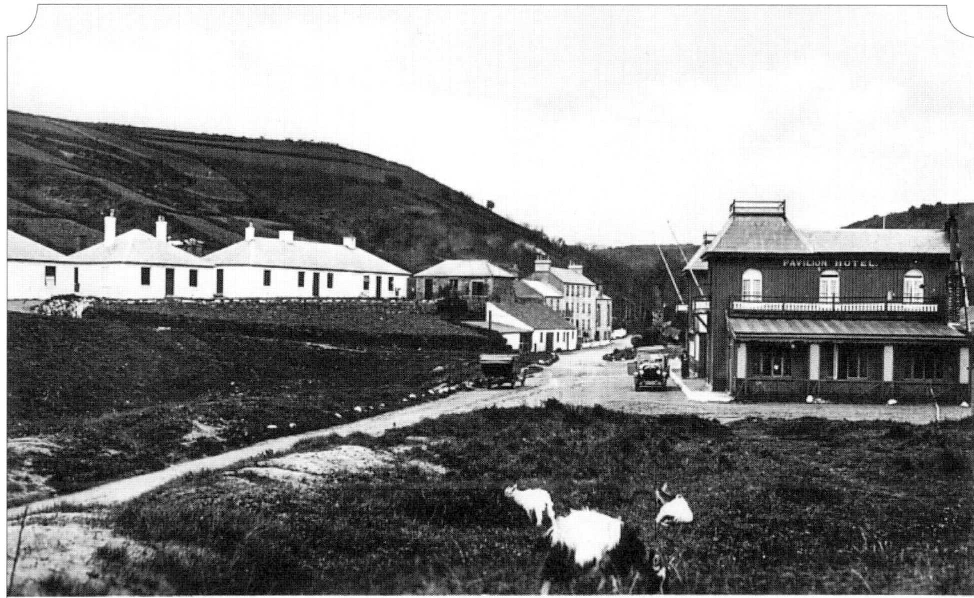

L 106 OLD BARRACKS AND PAVILION HOTEL, GREVE-DE-LECQ, JERSEY.

The Prince of Wales hotel survives to the west side of the bay. On another post-card the hotel proprietor has hand-written on the back as follows:

'Terms with board
August 55/- July 49/-
Other months 45/-
weekly each person.
Late dinner. Sep tables
Electric light throughout.
Modern sanitation.
Comfortable lounge
Dining room overlooks the bay - a sea view with all meals.
Accommodation for 20 guests only.'

This postcard is undated but it is likely to be some time between the wars. The Pavilion Hotel was a handsome and characterful building until it burnt down in the mid-1970s. It was replaced by Caesar's Palace, perhaps aimed mainly at tourists, which itself was replaced with 'traditional' residential development.

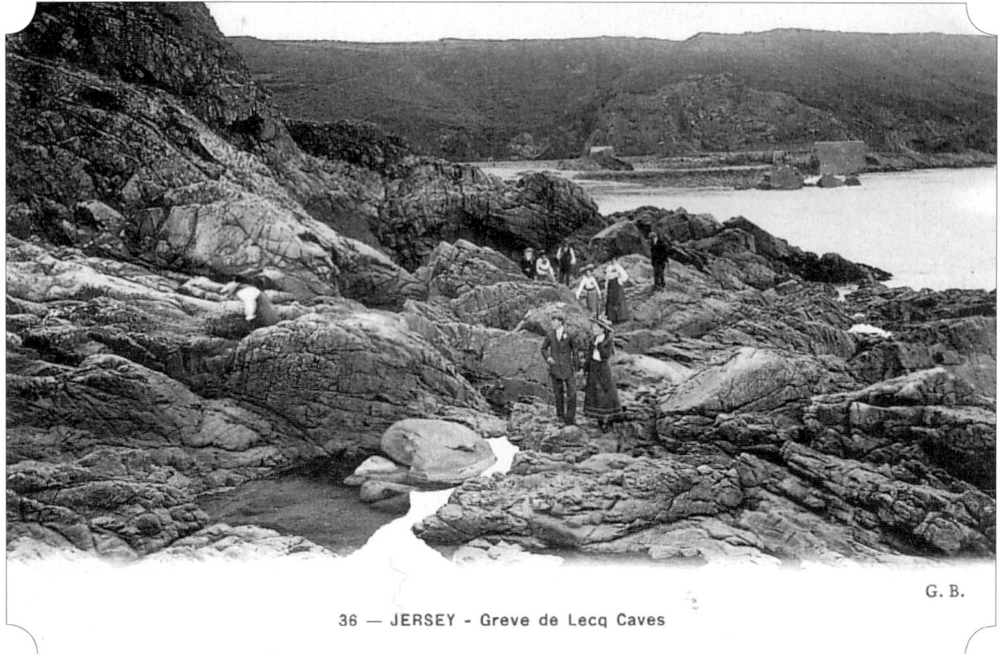

Message from 1936:

'We have just paddled and watched the others bathe. Alas we are too sore to bathe ourselves, the sun has treated us very badly. Isn't Grève de Lacq pretty - we're thoroughly enjoying ourselves here.'

Intrepid Edwardians exploring the rocks on the east side of the bay, long skirts no disincentive for the ladies!

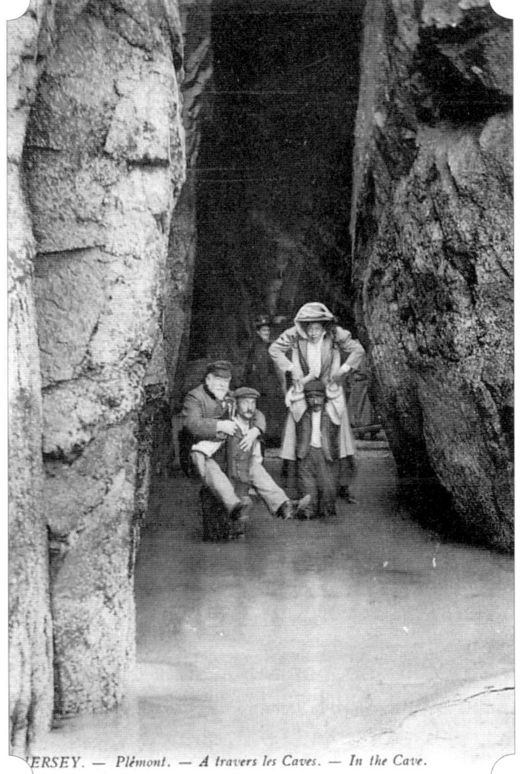
JERSEY. — Plémont. — A travers les Caves. — In the Cave.

Two postcards, reduced in size, of the caves at Plémont. Local porters were employed to carry the visitors and prevent them getting wet. In the picture on the left, two local men, with flat caps and trim moustaches, look a good deal slighter than their charges. And neither do they wear any protection from the cold seawater. Note how the lady is carried – the bearer has his arms thrust beneath the lady's armpits, in contrast to the picture on the right.

It is said that, if the receding tide did not leave many deep pools, then the porters would dig them out to ensure their services were required by the next arrival of visitors.

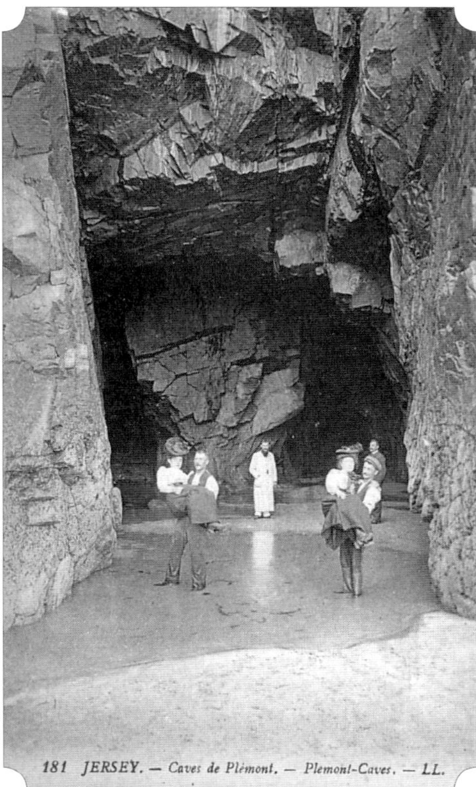
181 JERSEY. — Caves de Plémont. — Plemont-Caves. — LL.

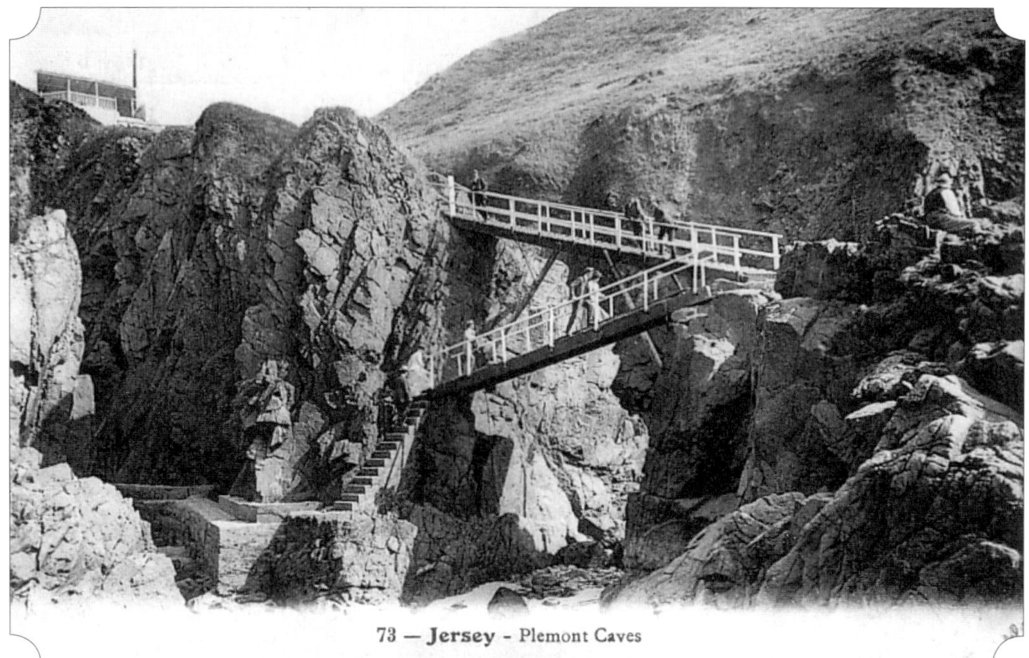

73 — **Jersey** - Plemont Caves

'This afternoon we have been for a drive at Plemont & have had our tea at the little picnic house which you can see [top left, opposite]. We have already lost ourselves a few times. Will have a few things to tell you when I come back.

Au revoir, Frank'

~

Message to Mr & Mrs Peel of Helenborough, Scotland, 1951:

'This is an ideal place for a holiday. Continual sunshine, 1st class Hotel & French cooking - we must all come here.'

Access to the beach at Plémont was, and remains, via sloping bridges and steps, though not quite by the arrangement seen here. Visitors remain attracted here by the dramatic caves which bore into the dominant cliffs behind a superb beach which is covered at high tide.

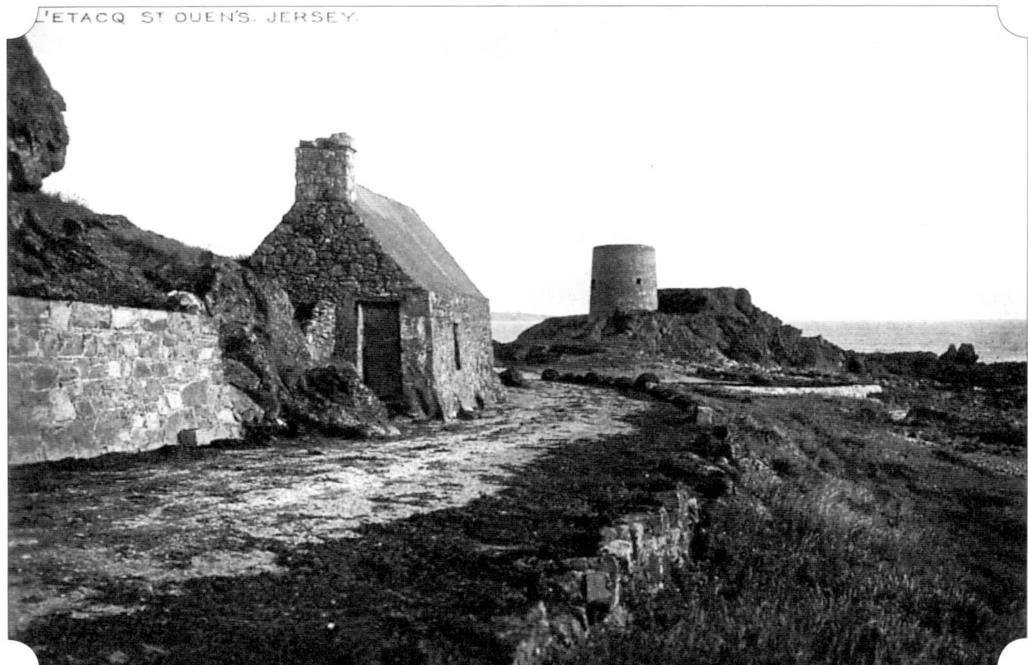

A postcard to Miss Brown of Chiswick, London, in 1949:

'We have had a most perfect week, but a week does not really warrant the journey. We have completely toured the coast of the island. Everything brown instead of green under the very hot sun and nearly all the inhabitants speaking French (a patois thereof) amongst themselves.'

The road just above the beach at L'Etacq. Going south it reaches St Ouen's Bay while going north it climbs to Les Landes and the elevated road along the north coast.

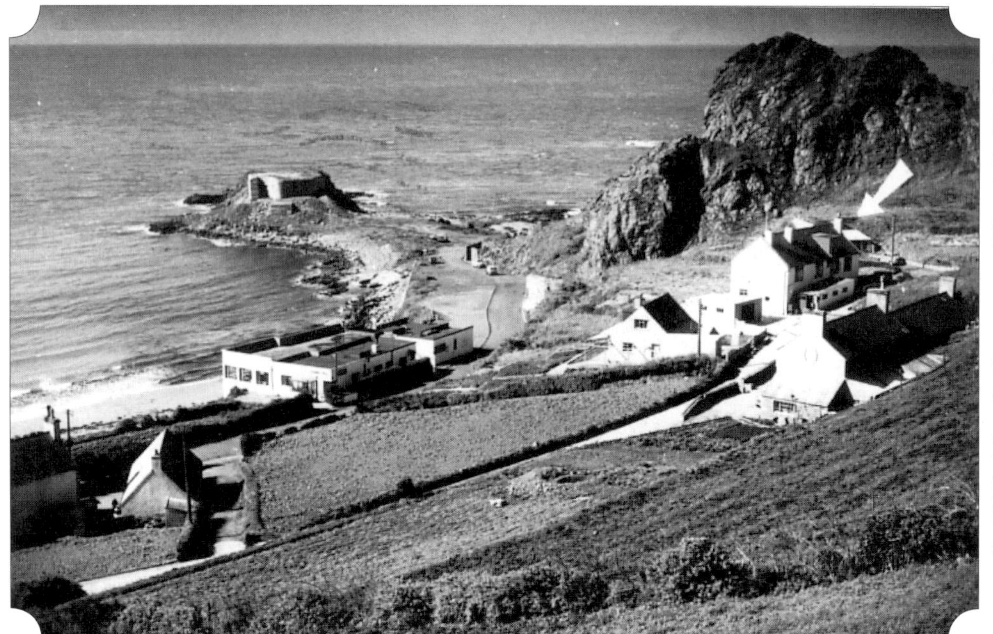

This postcard looks north-west from Jersey's north-west corner. It features L'Etacquerel Guest House, indicated by a bold white arrow.The former Marina Bars can be seen above the beach, now replaced with a row of dwellings.

Message sent in 1935:

'I'm having a lovely time over here, it's a beautiful place, & so much to see. Cigarettes 20 for 4d, beer 4d pint, in fact we just LIVE. Weather is hot & I'm bathing every day.'

~

Another message:

'This will be the last card from Jersey - yesterday was lovely, today pouring again - but we have just got to accepting it now. Think we have put on weight.'

~

And another:

'Jersey is lovely though the crossing was foul. I succumbed to the movement of the waves.'

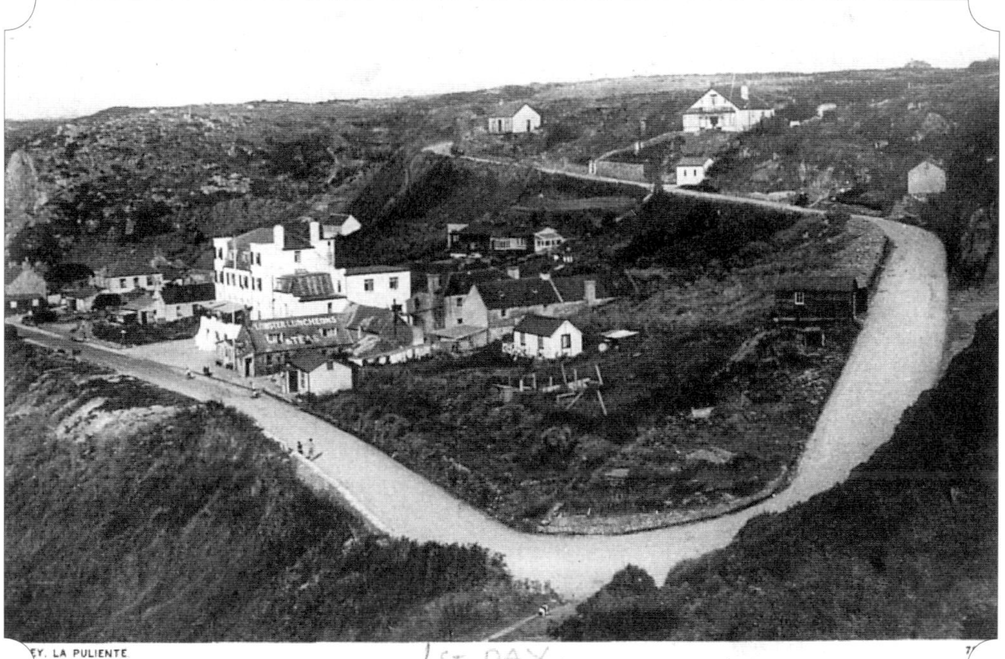

La Pulente, at the southern end of St Ouen's Bay. The roof of the single-story building below the major white building, now La Pulente pub, declares in large letters: 'LOBSTER LUNCHEONS'

To Mrs J Hawkins of Hammersmith, London:

'This will be the last card from Jersey - yesterday was lovely, today pouring again - but we have just got to accepting it now. Think we have put on weight.
Eileen'

~

Message to Mr & Mrs Clark of Rottingdean, Sussex on a card postmarked 21st August, 1951:

'Still enjoying life here. All looking like niggers. Feel I could stay another week, but all good things come to an end. All the best to all, Dollie'

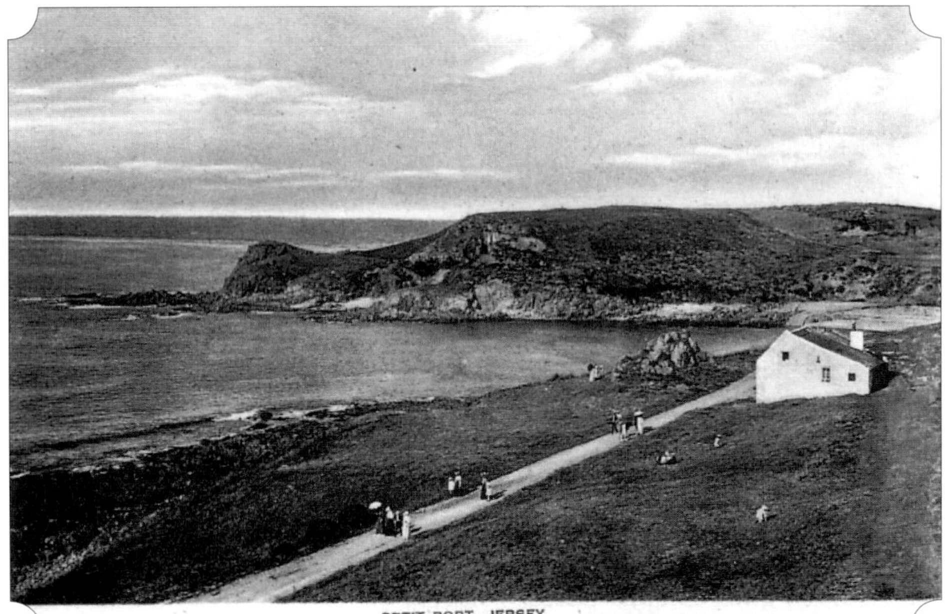

View of folk promenading along the south side of Petit Port, an inlet between St Ouen's Bay and Corbière.

A postcard sent in 1954 to Mr & Mrs Fenwick of Wembley, Middlesex, bore the following message:

'Having a very happy time. Weather just to our liking. Both enjoyed plane journey & have finished coming by sea as saving of time makes such a difference. We are both feeling very refreshed and well. This time next week back to usual routine. We leave Thurs 3.15. I think one pint of milk & a small loaf will do.'

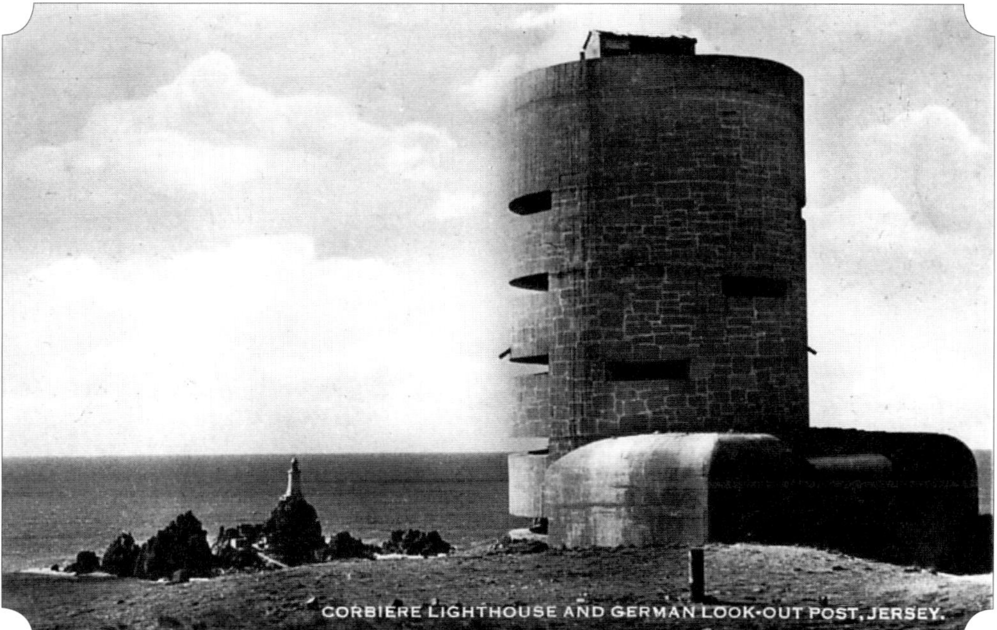

CORBIERE LIGHTHOUSE AND GERMAN LOOK-OUT POST, JERSEY.

Corbière Lighthouse and German Look-Out Post. In this view the lighthouse is dwarfed by the later structure which the German occupiers attempted to disguise as a granite building.

To Mr Wetherill of High Wycombe, 1952:

Dear Mum & Dad
What tobacco do you want?
Reply al speed.
Norman'

~

From a postcard without a postmark but, judging by the message, sent soon after the Liberation. Sent to Miss Roche in Wolverhampton:

'We had a very rough crossing. Both very ill. Visiting relatives most of the time so far. they have had a dreadful time. They can't really believe that it is all over.'

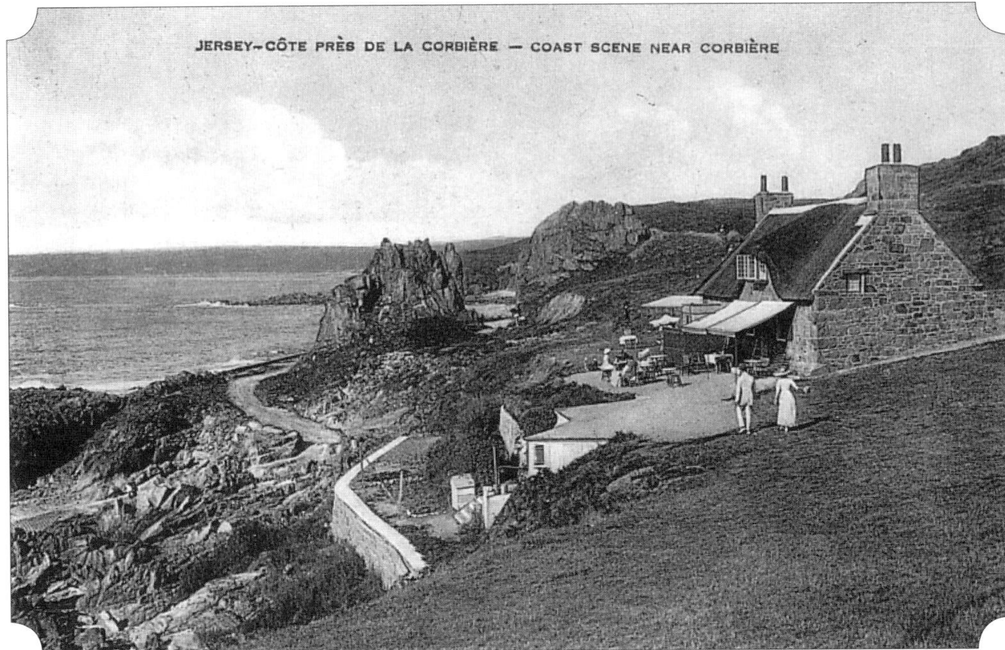

View of Corbière, but without its famous lighthouse.

To Miss Stanpool of Stockbridge, 1946:

'Had a lovely day on a farm yesterday, plenty to eat, the bread and cakes are much nicer than ours.

Love Lilian'

~

Message to Mrs Barker of Dartford, Kent, sent in 1932:

'Dear Mother,
We are stranded in a lighthouse owing to the rain. It turned out lovely yesterday. We have fine lodgings, the lady of the house is young & ever such a sport. I shouldn't be surprised if it doesn't stop raining all the holiday.'

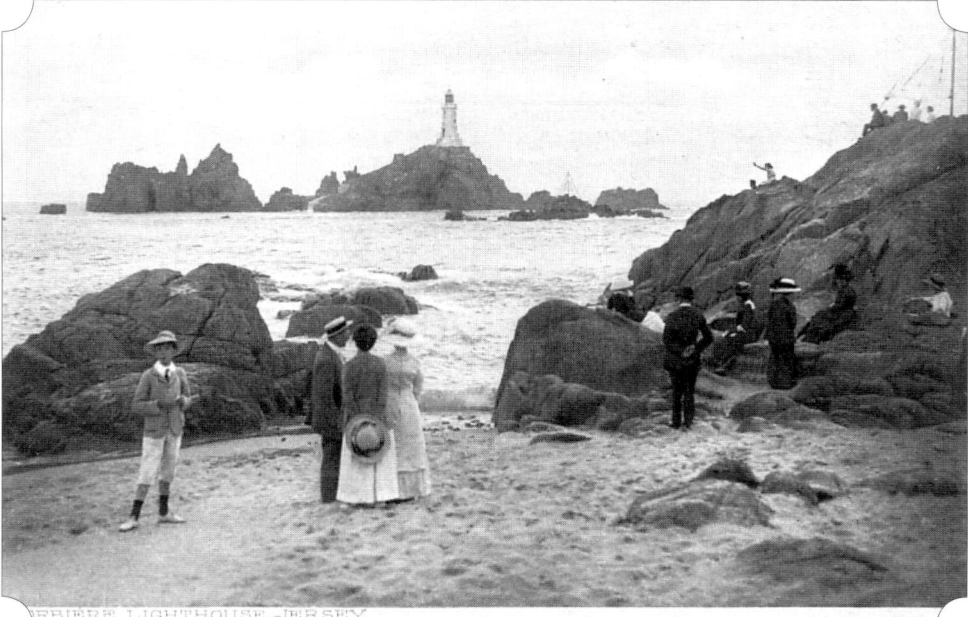

From a guide bood in 1927: 'No visit to Jersey is complete unless La Corbière is visited; there are frequent trains; those desiring to walk part of the way should alight at La Haule Station, and walk up La Haule Hill, one of the prettiest roads in Jersey, with its cuttings through rock and overhanging trees. Cyclists and those driving or motoring should also take this road.'

To Miss Simpson of Edinburgh, 4th March, 1912:

'Am seeing as much of the island as I can. Going to see Corbière lighthouse this afternoon. A very wild part there. Having a good time & sorry to leave so soon.

Love Fred'

~

A postcard sent in 1909, and addressed to Miss Jenny Young of Innerleithen, Scotland:

'We came on here today from St Malo. The island is lovely. Ideal place for a honeymoon. I said so! So note this down! Weather is mid-summer broiling hot. Nevertheless we are fairly active and mean to see (comfortably) what is to be seen.'

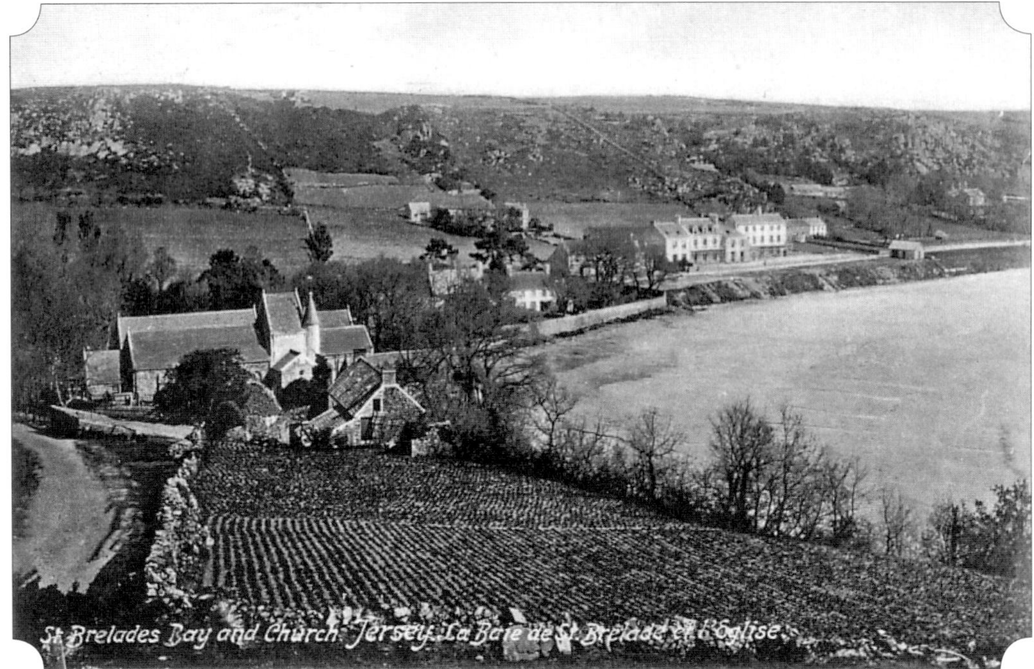

View across the western corner of St Brelade's Bay featuring the parish church in the left foreground, the only one of Jersey's twelve parish churches with a sea view. Here too is the ancient Fishermen's Chapel with its fascinating frescoes.

To Mr & Mrs W of Wanstead, London, in 1954:

'Dear All
Havng a grand time. Weather is excellent. The Hotel is very good with plenty to eat. Drinks & cigs are cheap, so we are making the most of it. Fkying to Guernsey next week for a day.

Ray & Molly'

~

To Miss M Sanders of Bristol, 11th June, 1051:

'We arrived quite safely. The boat trip was lovely and the others enjoyed the plane journey. The weather is good & the hotel all that could be desired. We like it on the island very much.'

Yours sincerely, F. Phillips

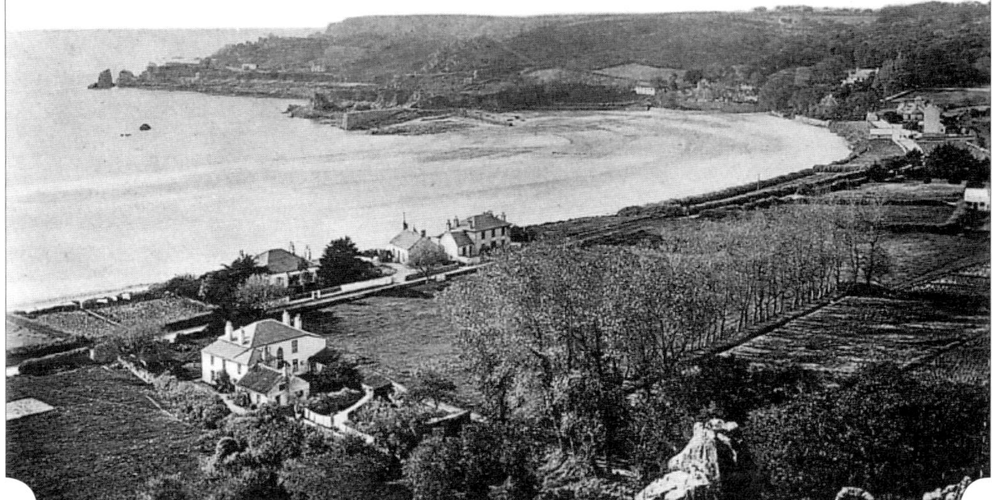

St Brelade's Bay, for many years perhaps Jersey's most popular, though in this view in a rather less developed state than today.

Message sent to O Smith Esq. of South Godsatone, Surrey, 11th May, 1931:

My dear Dad,

Although I have only just begun my holiday, I am having quite a good time. So far the weather is behaving well, but not quite up to scratch yet. You'd love Jersey, it's very beautiful, and the sea so blue, but you want to be a good walker to reap the full benefit. Already I have walked a long way, but there's so much to see, you forget about being tired. I went to this little bay on Saturday afternoon, can you imagine stretches of golden sand, surrounded with deep blue water, & rugged rocks, & in the background hills covered with yellow gorse, it's a picture. I've met some very nice people at the Hotel, but we are only 12 in all.

Heaps of love, Evie

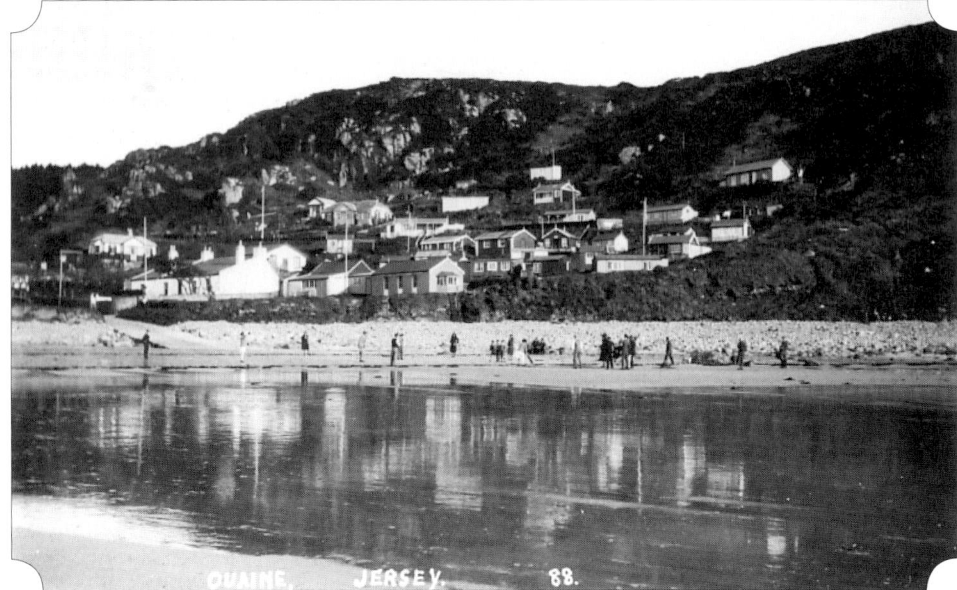

Ouaisné Bay (the Jersey place name which contains all five vowels: a, e, i, o, and u). Shack-like dwellings, now largely replaced, nicely reflected in the wet sand. Postmarked 7th September, 1934, and addressed to Monsieur & Madame Picard in Rouen, France.

From a postcard dated 12th September, 1962:

'Dear Friends,
Just to let you know we arrived safely. Having a wonderful holiday. Did a coach trip all around the Island. All the different bays and beaches are wonderful, the Glass Church, and all the fortifications from the German Occupation. See you Sunday.'

~

To Miss N Simm of Bournemouth in 1934:

'We passed this today [Portelet] and are at present sat in the rocks almost like an armchair only of course without the cushions. We have done a good deal of cliimbing and scrambling.
Love from May'

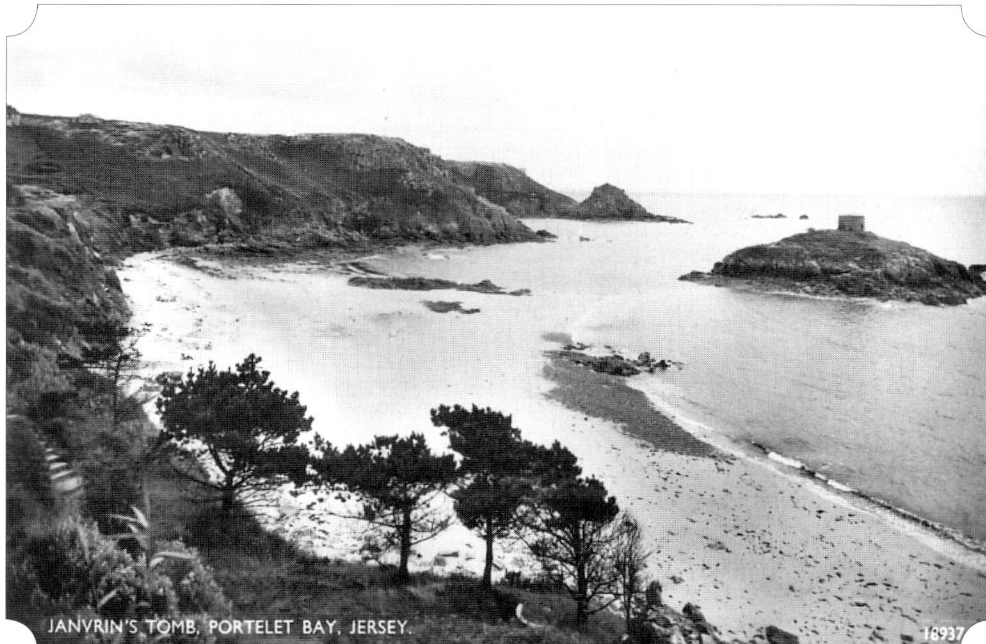

From Ward Lock's Gide, 1937: 'The increasing popularity of Portelet is evidenced by the rapidly increasing number of bungalows and hoiday camps, where, away from all charabanc routes, visitors can dress as they please and lead the simple life.'

Posted to Manchester in 1946, the first tourist season following the Liberation. The correspondent is mindful of rationing at home, as the message implies:

'Portelet Bay Holiday Camp
Jersey, C.I.

Dear Mrs & Mr Ramsden,
Just a few lines to let you know that Betty and I are experiencing very good weather and having an extremely enjoyable time. The food here is good, plentiful, and well cooked; accommodation clean and comfortable, and scenery delightful. Fruit is scarce, but we manage with strawberries, raspberries, cherries and ice cream, and of course unlimited tomatoes. We shall be sorry when the time to depart is due. Cheerio for now and kindest regards.

Bill & Betty'

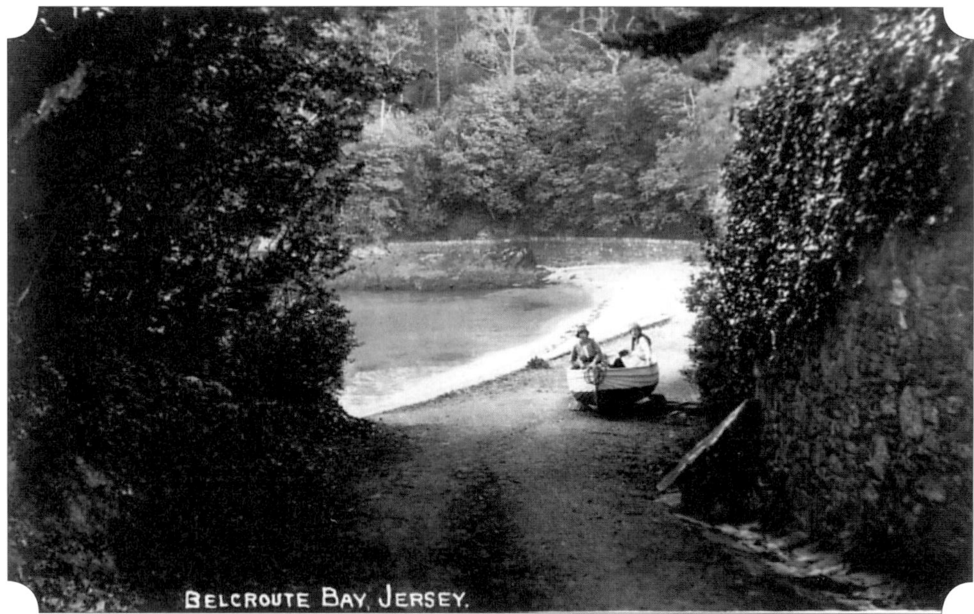

Belcroute Bay is one of Jersey's less frequented coastal spots, though it looks fairly idyllic in this view.

To Mrs Battrick of Manchester:

'Biarritz Hotel
24.9.64

Despite warning of strong head winds resulting in longer flight times arrived at airport at 12.30. It's absolutely tropical here - backless cotton frocks in the drawing room & sun worshippers lying along the balcony looking like walnuts (in colour!). I don't know if I told you that this hotel is a Methodist Holiday Home & seems full. I think you would like it here. Sorry about the bad writing - new biro seems to make me wobble! Regards to all.'

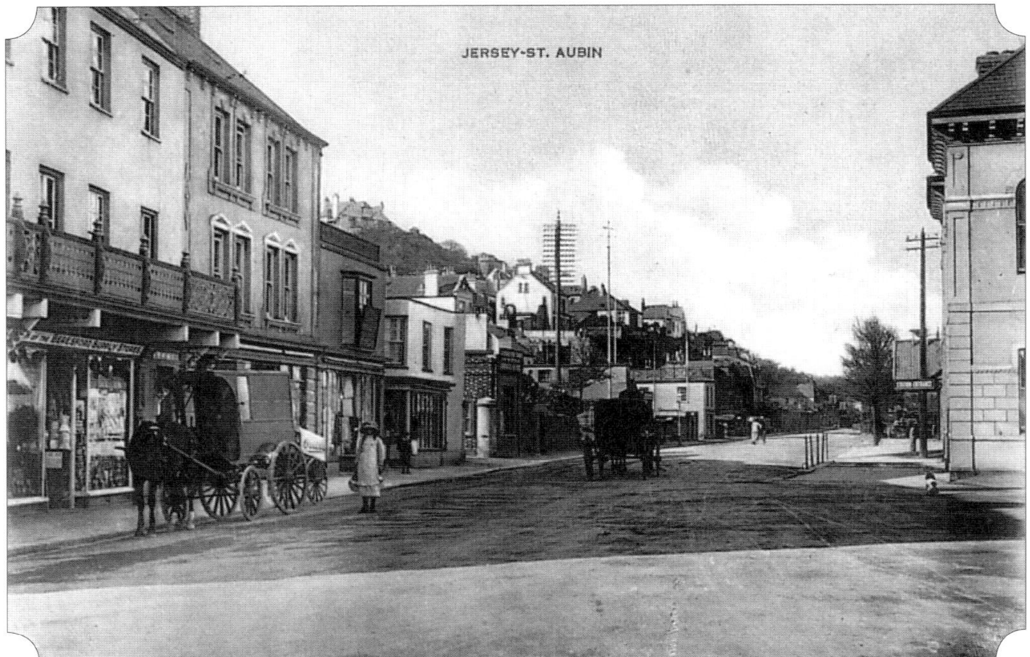

St Aubin before the age of the car. Note the sign outside the former railway station on the right which reads STATION ENTRANCE. Also the grocery shop on the left BERESFORD SUPPLY STORES. This became ORVISS, then LE RICHE, then STAMPERS and is now CHECKERS XPRESS.

'Enjoying our holiday very much so hot in lovely sun. Have found a spot very like Wales for isolation but lovely beach. We have taken to cycling and are getting round very well now the wind has dropped.

Yrs. Betty'

~

Message from a postcard dated 1st August 1952:

'Having a great holiday here. Saw the Battle of Flowers yesterday and it was marvellous. Everything parched as they have had very little rain since April.'

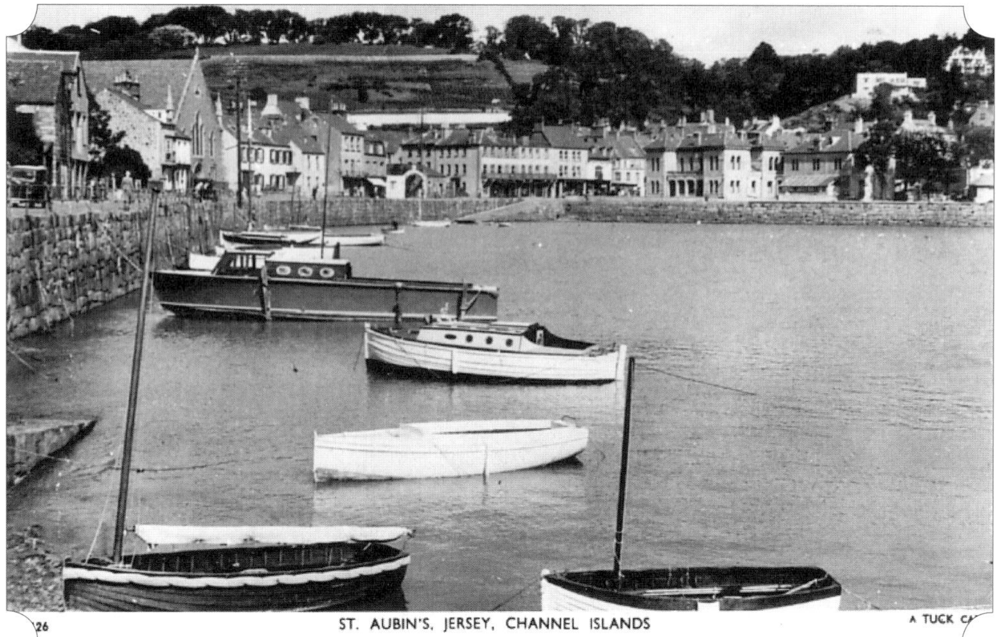

View of an uncrowded St Aubin's Harbour.

The card shown on this page is postmarked 8th August, 1956 and bears the following message:

Dear Mr & Mrs B
We are having a wonderful time. The weather has been glorious. It's been about 80° today. Hope you have a nice time.

Yours sincerely, DHR

~

Message from a postcard sent in 1952 to Mr & Mrs Butler of Itchen, Southampton:

'Dear Mom & Pop,
Well we arrived here dead tired 5.30 this morning. The place is very nice, food good so far and what a lovely bedroom. Cliff is in heaven just shorts on sun-bathing after a swim.

Love Beryl xxx'

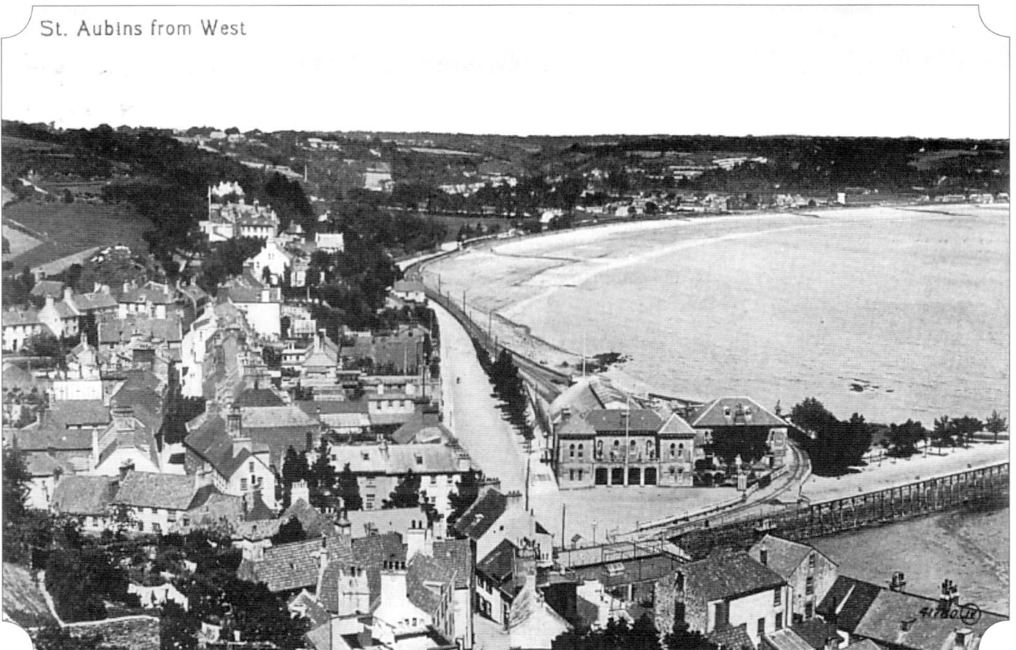

The card was posted on 8th August, 1914, four days after the declaration of World War I and addressed to Mr E Hancock in Dorchester, Dorset. The message reads:

'Dear Cousin
I am very sorry I was unable to call on Friday evening, as I was on the rush until Sat. to catch the boat. It is nothing but war here.'

This postcard, with its view of St Aubin from the west, illustrates the railway track as it approaches St Aubin's Station (formerly the Terminus Hotel and now St Brelade's Parish Hall) and the Corbière line to the right making a sharp right-hand bend.

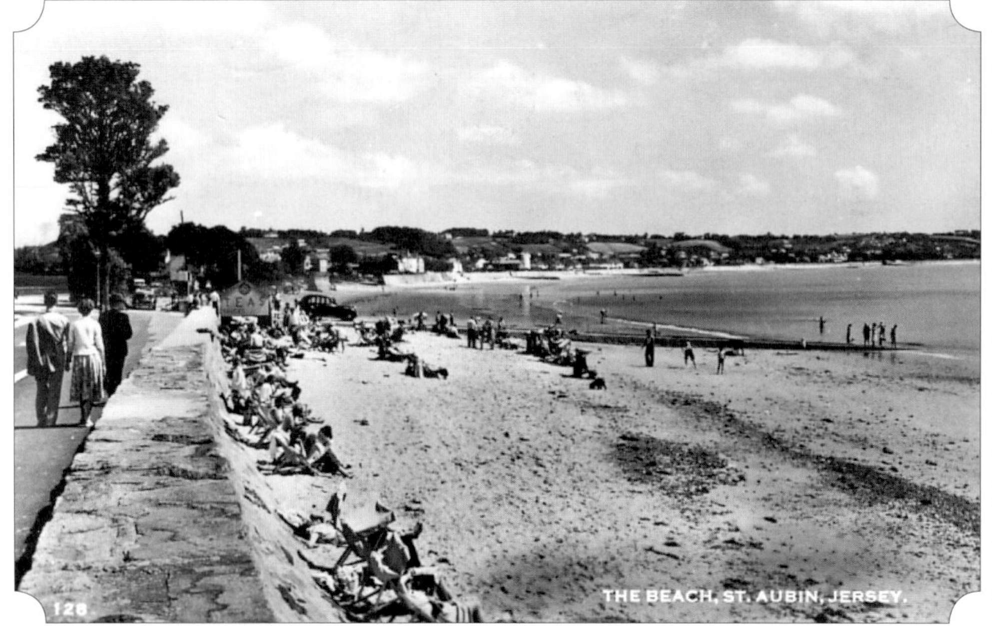

A view approaching La Haule slipway in the busy summer months. It is unlikely to be as crowded nowadays but still a lovely beach and an ideal place to head for to get away from the crowds.

The following message was written, not by a visitor, but by a local, so not strictly within the scope of this book, but nevertheless worth quoting. It is addressed to Mr & Mrs G of Havant, Hampshire:

'Looking at snaps taken in '38 reminds me you might be at this address. Am here on Aug. 7th. Leave after 7 years at home 6 Cheapside, St Helier. All at Cheapside well considering Jean & Clem quite grown up, new addition to family, Carol age 4 yrs cute blond thing. Weather still as perfect as ever but poor island looking very delapidated after 5 years occupation, most Bays ruined. Arthur & Frankie send best regards. Hope you are both well, much love.

Betty

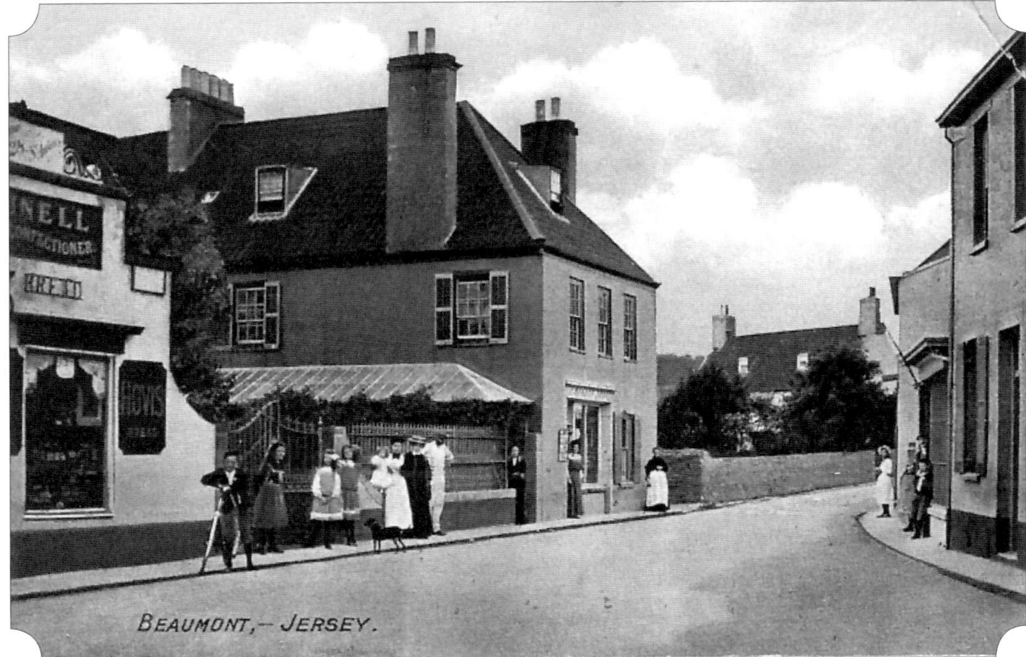

A postcard sent to Mr & Mrs M of Bedford carried the following message:

Arrived OK. This is a really lovely island. Weather scorching hot. We shall soon look like cooked lobsters. Smashing hotel - waiters are all Italian - good food. Things here are dirt cheap - beer 6d a pint - cigarettes 20 for 1/6d. The scenery here is absolutely marvellous - are having a really lovely time.
Love to you all. Pip & Geoff

Beaumont in quieter times. This is now the junction through which passes much of the traffic heading to and from the airport. Dunell's Bakery, with a HOVIS sign fixed to the wall, can be seen on the left.

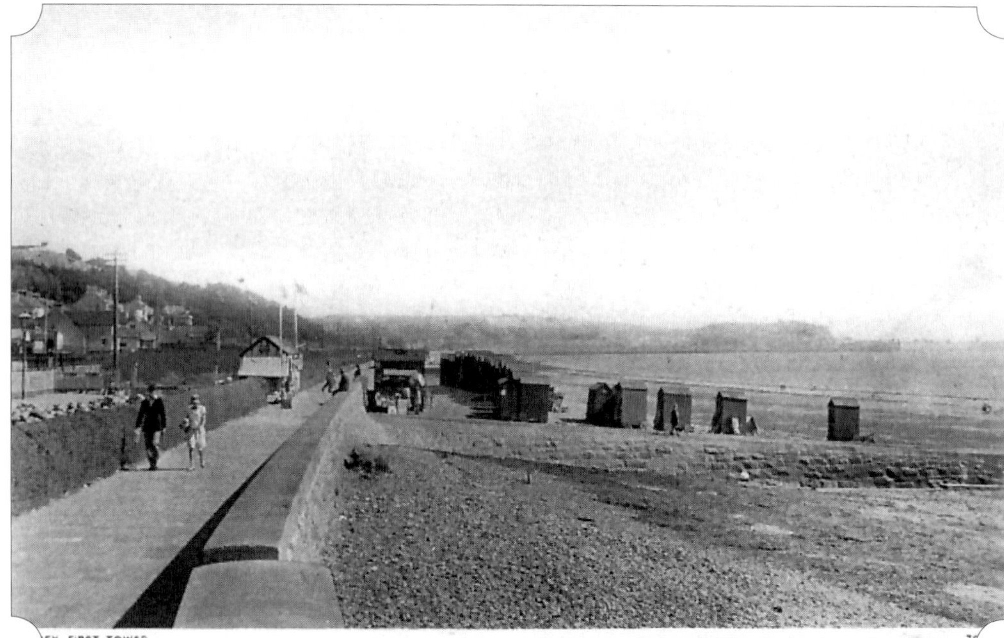

View east towards St Helier, the Harbour and Fort Regent. A number of bathing machines on the beach indicates this picture was produced in a more modest age.

Postmarked 2nd July, 1932 and addressed to Miss Collins of Teignmouth, Devon:

'Dear Mary
Shall be home late on Sat. night so will see you on Sun. unless taken ill in the meantime - doing my best to cope with too many late nights but no hopes.

Hilda'

~

Addressed to Miss C Stewart of Edinburgh and sent 27th August, 1935:

'Having a good holiday. Weather perfect. Plenty of fun. Was a bit sick on the boat coming but it was worth it all.

Vera'

~ Attractions ~

Jersey's major attractions, so far as the holidaymaker is concerned, include its climate (generally more favourable than the mainland), its beaches, coastline and countryside, together with its proximity to France and its consequent 'differentness' to British resorts. As if all this were not enough, a number of tourist attractions, of varied quality, developed throughout the rise of mass tourism in the last century.

Guide books consistently recommended tours of the island which took in the best of the coastal and inland scenery. A high point of these tours was a stop at Prince's Tower, which stood above La Hougue Bie and which afforded 'a good view from the top over about two-thirds of the Island'. The Prince's Tower was demolished shortly after the excavation of La Hougue Bie and the discovery that it is a prehistoric site of major importance.

One of the foremost attractions of pre-war days was the so-called Troglodyte Caves at Five Oaks. A guide book in 1921 comments, a touch reservedly: 'Troglodyte Caves is an instance of what can be done with shells, stones, a little lake and a few mud walls. Some visitors find a quaint interest here, others are amused, and others again are not.'

During the heyday of the 1950s there were three main attractions to which the motor coaches carried visitors: the Glass Church at Millbrook, the German Underground Hospital in St Peter's and the German Occupation Museum at La Hougue Bie. And that was about it until the opening of many others in later years, like Jersey Zoo and the Lavender Farm. Jersey Museums have latterly done a wonderful job of presenting the rich and varied strands of the island's history in an informative, entertaining and highly professional manner at various historic sites around the island.

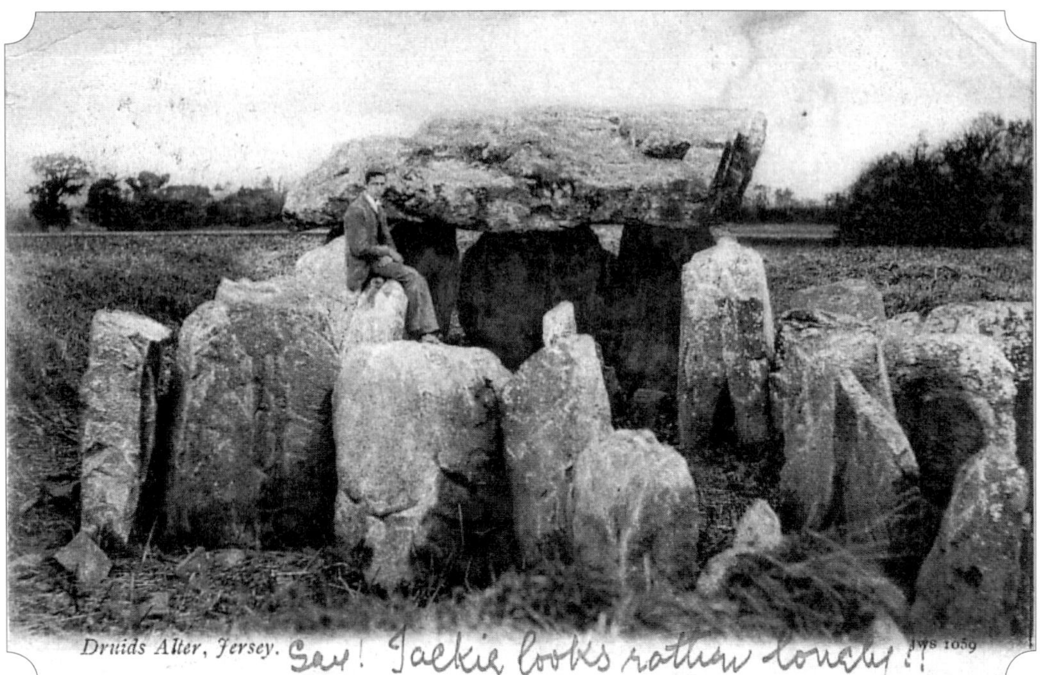

The postcard shown here is captioned 'Druids Alter'. It is not a "Druids Alter' at all, or even a 'Druids' Altar'; this is a dolmen, or burial chamber, which would once have been covered in earth so as to appear as a great mound.
It is postmarked 24th August, 1904, and addressed to Miss Drew of Holborn, London:

'Dear Glad,
Am having a very nice time. Weather lovely - plenty of "Francair" but do not want any of them. Nearly all fellows in the house.

Love May'

Jersey possesses several impressive prehistoric dolmens or burial chamblers. They were constructed during the New Stone Age between 4800 and 2250 BC and are in varying states of preservation and have long been accessible to the public.

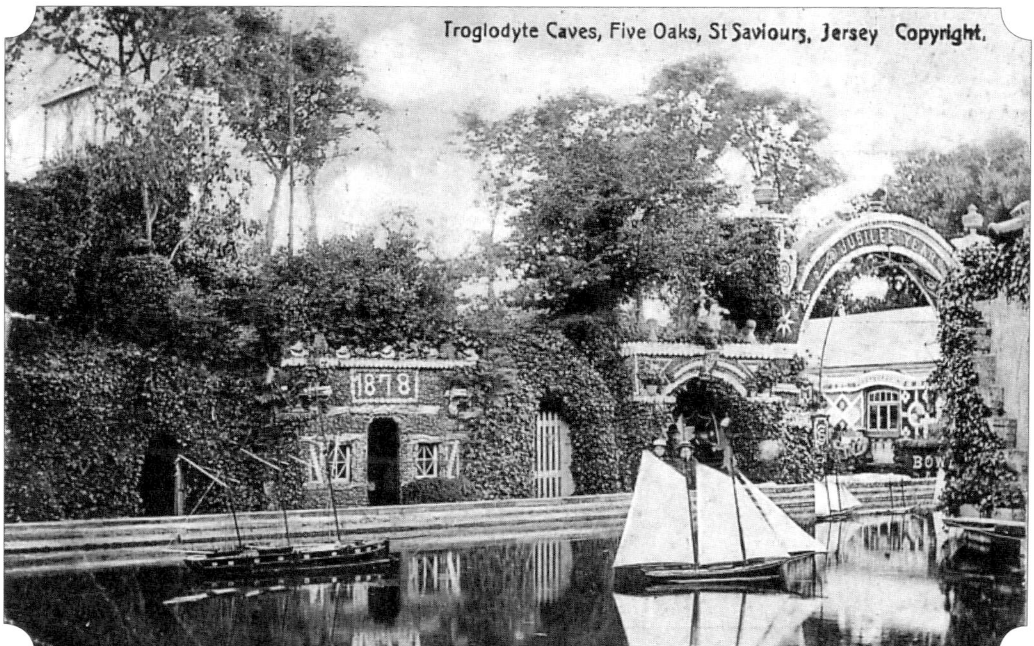

Message from a postcard dated 1st August 1952:

'Having a great holiday here. Saw the Battle of Flowers yesterday and it was marvellous. Everything parched as they have had very little rain since April.'

~

From 1952:

'Dear Mum & Dad
What tobacco do you want? Reply all speed.
Norman'

'Troglodyte Caves, Five Oaks, are well worth a visit. Here are to be seen a series of small caves skilfully lined with shells, as well as ornamental waters and nicely-kept grounds; the whole reflecting great credit upon the perseverence and patience of the proprietor. Music and refershments are both provided.' – *guide book, 1899*

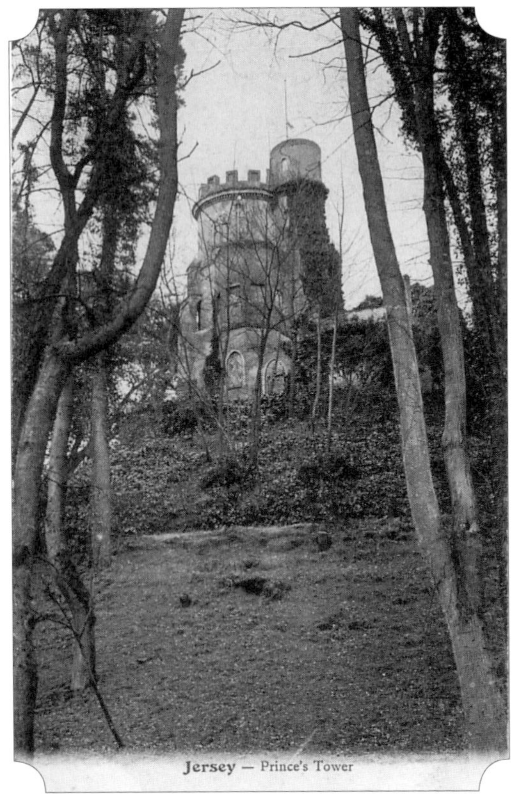
Jersey — Prince's Tower

Two postcards, reduced in size, of Prince's Tower, St Martin's, erected towards the end of the 18th century. Used as an observation post during the French Wars, it formerly surmounted the chapel on the summit of the mound known as La Hougue Bie. Demolished in 1924, the Prince's Tower, with its magnificent views over much of the island, was once a magnet for every visitor to Jersey.

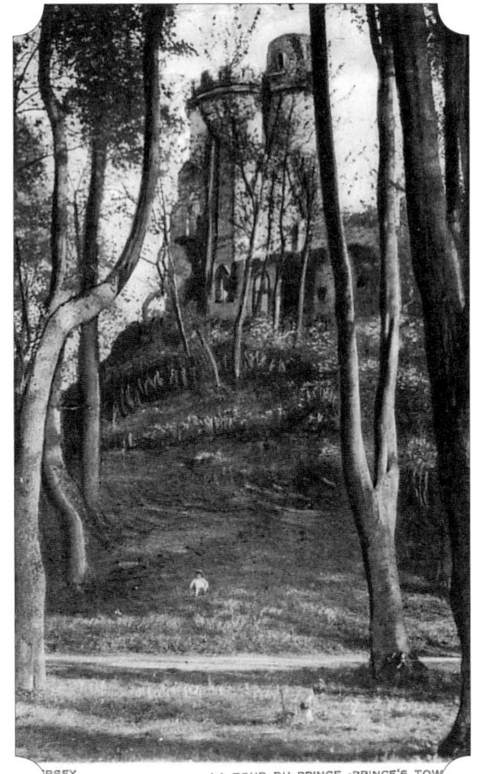
RSEY LA TOUR DU PRINCE -PRINCE'S TOW

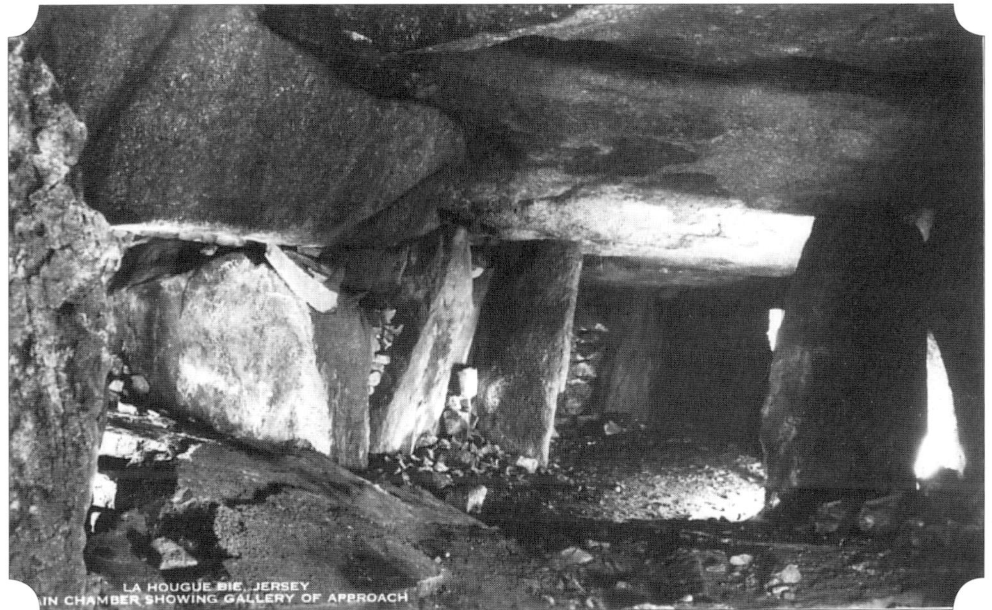

Message to Mr Taylor of Sunderland, 1935:

'Dear Lummy
The telephones here seem to be hopeless at night. I tried to get through Sunday but it was no use.'

~

And one to Mrs W Andrews of Croydon:

'The weather is really grand here in fact we look like a couple of roast chickens already.

Love Ruth'

Since 1919, La Hougue Bie – claimed to be the finest dolmen in Western Europe, has been explored by the Société Jersiaise, though its archaeological significance was not realised until 1924. It is now open to the public under the auspices of the Jersey Museums Service, together with other attractions at the same site.

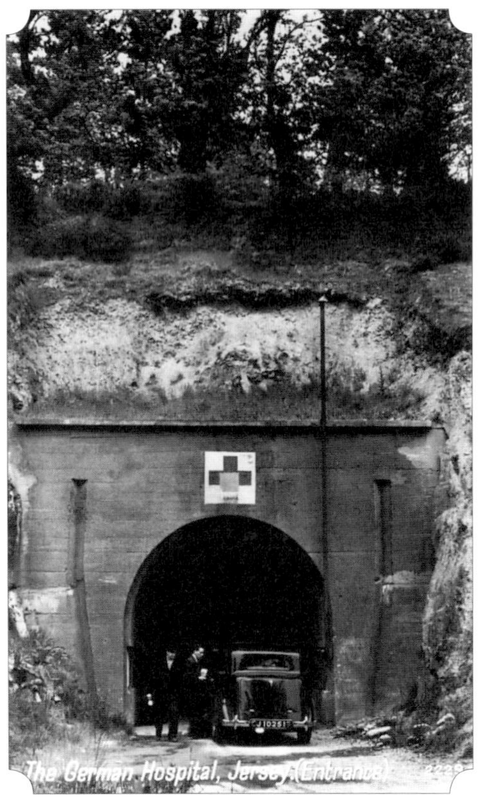

German Underground Hospital: Countless thousands of holidaymakers have visited here since it opened to the public. It was stripped of the majority of its fixtures and fittings soon after the Liberation, no doubt in a desire to get rid of everything connected with those five dark years. It remained a largely empty and rather spooky place for many years, and not particularly edifying for the visitor.

However, in latter years it gradually filled with exhibits relating to the Occupation; then, as Jersey War Tunnels, with displays concerning the Second World War in general.

(Two portrait postcards reduced in size)

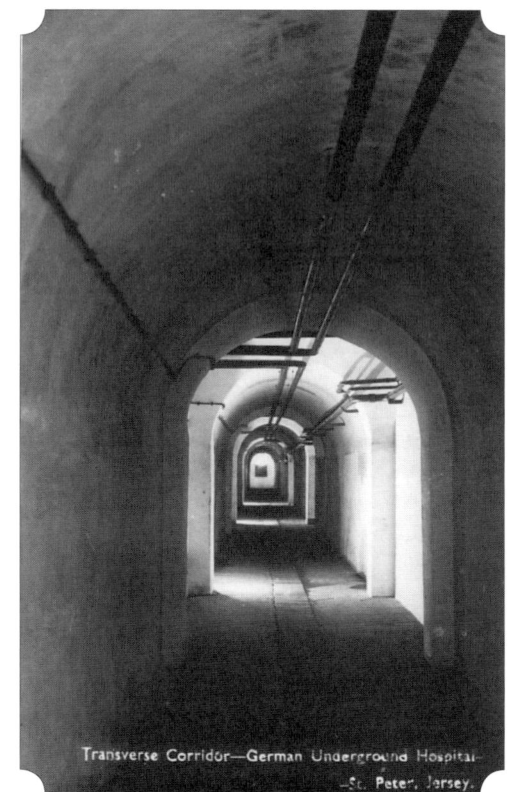

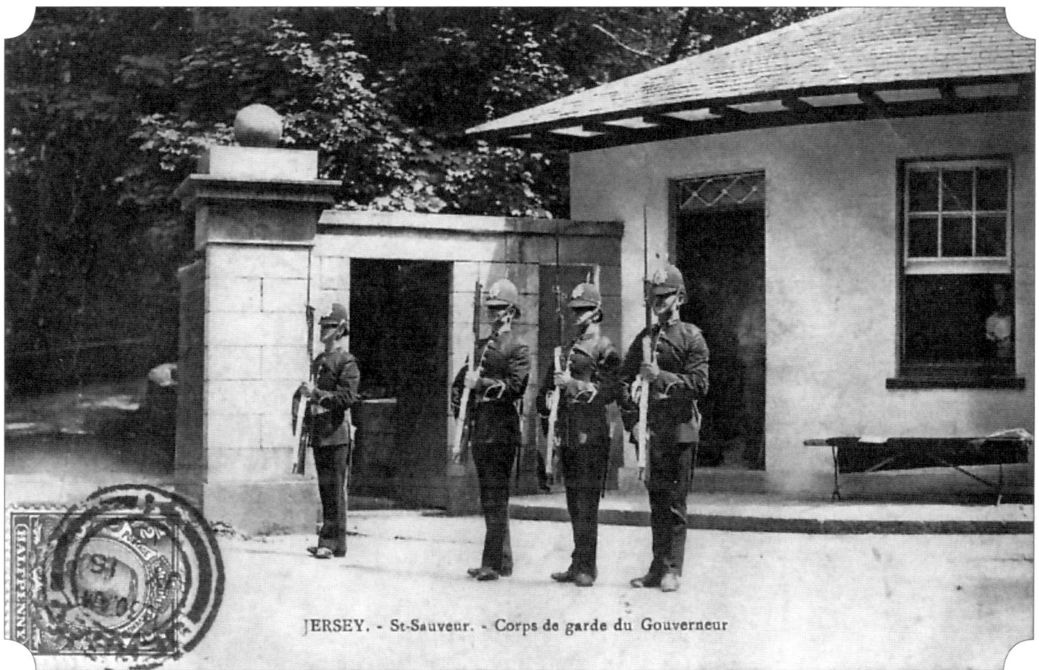

Message on card sent in 1947 to Rev & Mrs A Simmons in Halifax:

'Dear Auntie Hilda & Uncle Albert,
Just a hurried card to tell you how grand I have found your old home. I expect you would find a lot of changes, however, the people are still A1 in spite of their troubles.

Michael'

'St Sauveur – Corps de Garde du Gouveneur' Guards, whose iniforms resemble those of policemen, outside the Governor's residence in St Saviour.

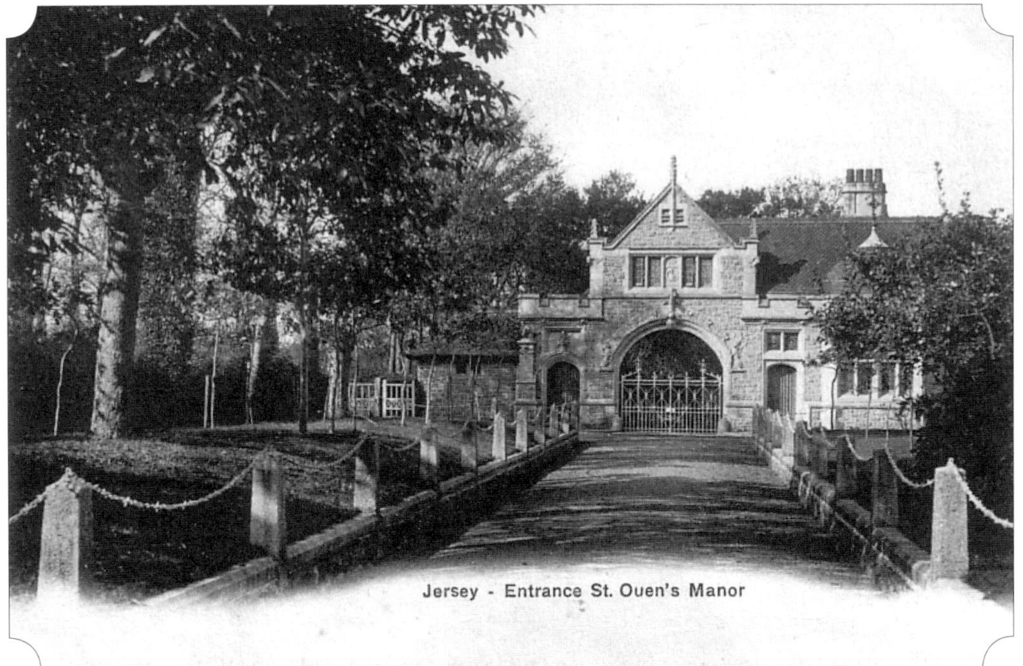

This is one of Jersey's several ancient manor houses. The grand entrance, shown here, is generally as far as visitors got.

Message from a postcard sent in 1956 and addrssed to Reception, Messrs. Knox & Hardy., London, EC4:

'Dear inmates,
Having a grand time (Don't wish you were here!!!) The hotel is a great place. We have got quite tanned especially the last few days. Hope everything's under control at your end and you are not working too hard. Don't let Mr B illtreat you.
Kind regards to all,
Cheerio, Audrey'

~

A message from 1947:

'Jersey is wonderful. We'll live here when we are old.'

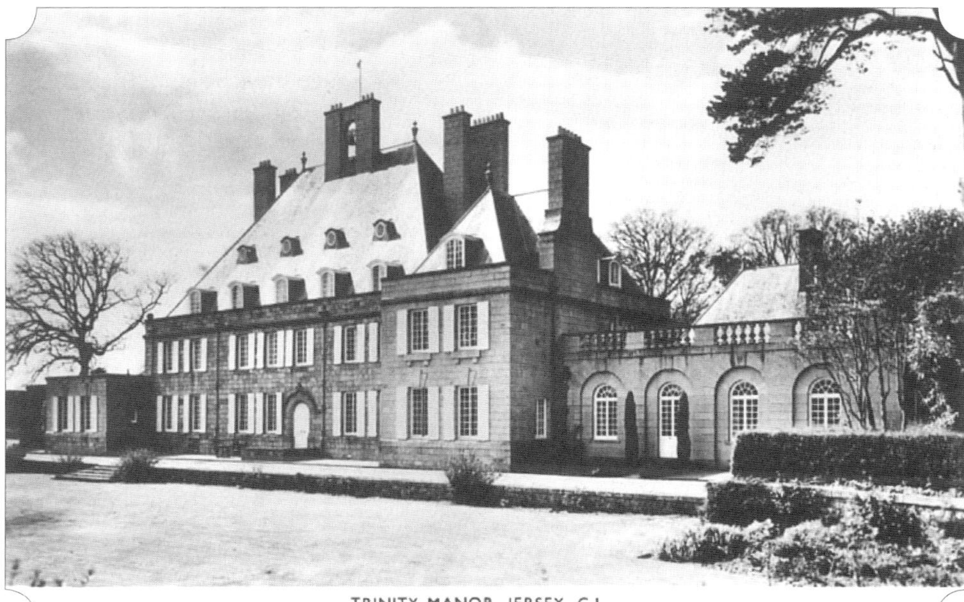

TRINITY MANOR, JERSEY, C.I.

Trinity Manor: An impressive pile and home to the Seigneur of the Trinity Parish. Not generally open to the public but visible from the road.

Message to Mrs Dewar of Ruislip, Middlesex, sent 4th September, 1933:

'Dear Mo
Arrived at 7.15, had a lovely trip across, the weather has been glorious. Roy has struck lucky, there is a boy his own age, no other children here. We went to a dance at the new Pavilion last night 8.30 until 12 o'clock. Sports tomorrow. Weather is still very hot. Love to all.

Clive'

~

To Miss R of Christchurch, Hampshire, 24th August, 1953:

'Had a fairly rough crossing and the sun seems to have deserted us. So have mostly gone shopping. We are having wonderful food so shall be really fat when we come home.

Bud'

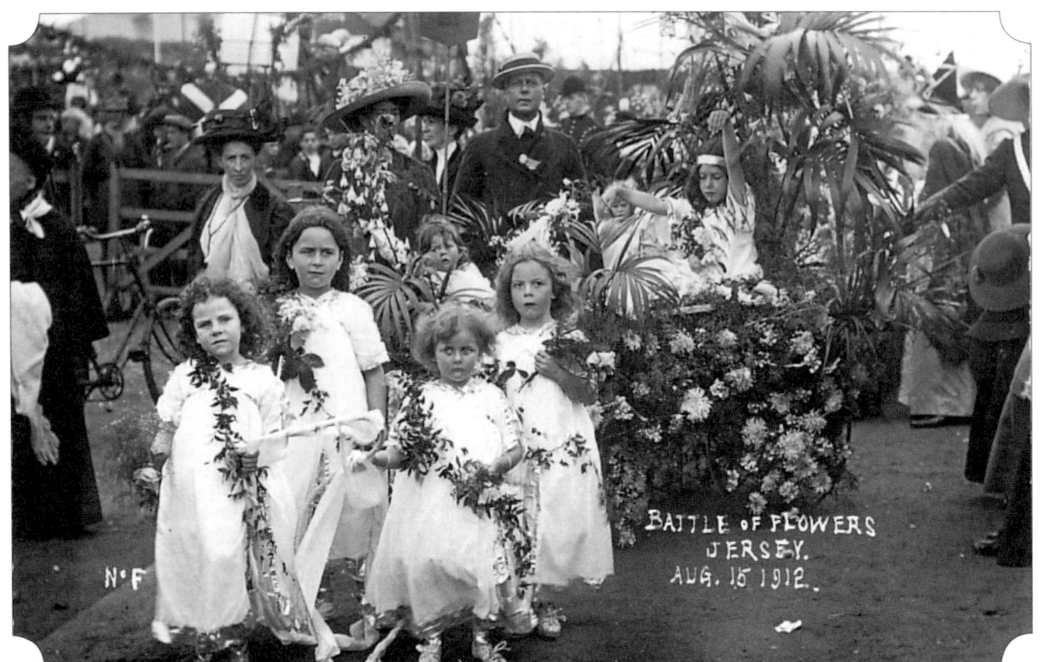

Message from a postcard sent 8th August, 1907 to Master W Bond of Wellington, Somerset:

'We are going to 'Battle of Flowers' a grand fete in front of West Park this afternoon when prizes are given for best decorated cars, vans, etc. Tons of flowers will be used on some of these devices & at conclusion they tear them off & throw at spectators on stands & vice versa – We go to Guernsey Sat morning leaving 9am'

The Battle of Flowers, an annual summer event which began in 1902. 'Spectacular Setting, Breathtaking Exhibits, Lavishly Decorated Arena, A real Spirit of Carnival' – from a guide book of 1955.

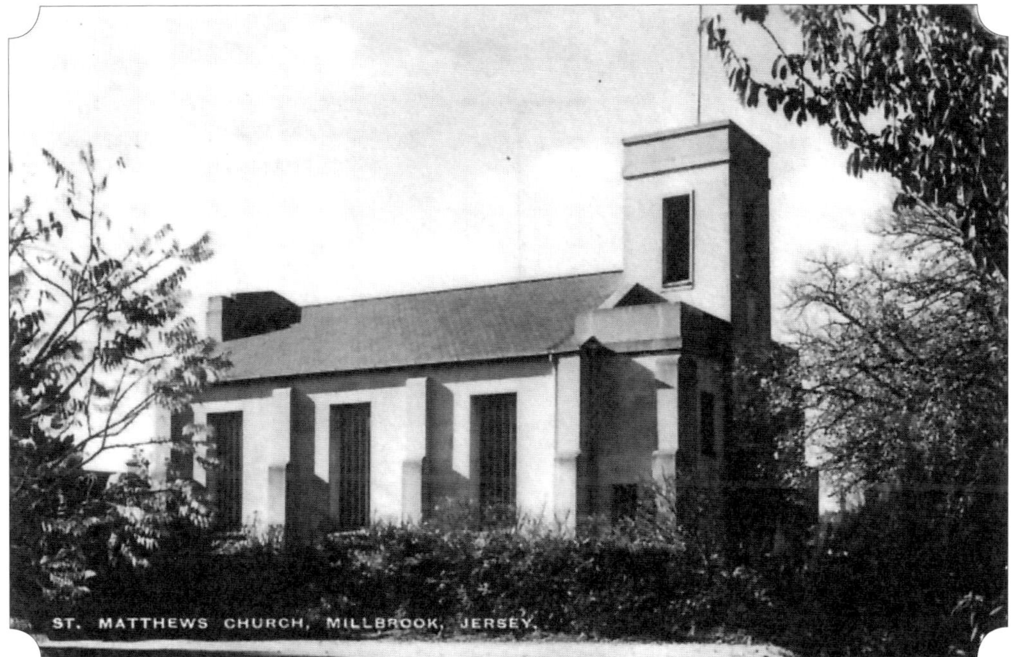

St Matthew's Church, Millbrook, St Lawrence: The church was reconstructed and rededicated in 1934 in memory of Lord Trent, founder of Boots the Chemists. Containing many features in Lalique glass, St Matthew's became known as 'The Glass Church'.

Message sent to Miss J Bracegirdle of Newbury, Berkshire, posted 29th August, 1950:

'Having grand time. Daddy & I went to service at the Church of Glass last Sunday. It was beautiful cannot express its beauty. We have just had a tour of the Island. We are just going in a party of 28 to the Esplanade. Table reserved by the Hotel.
Cheerio Love Mother xxx

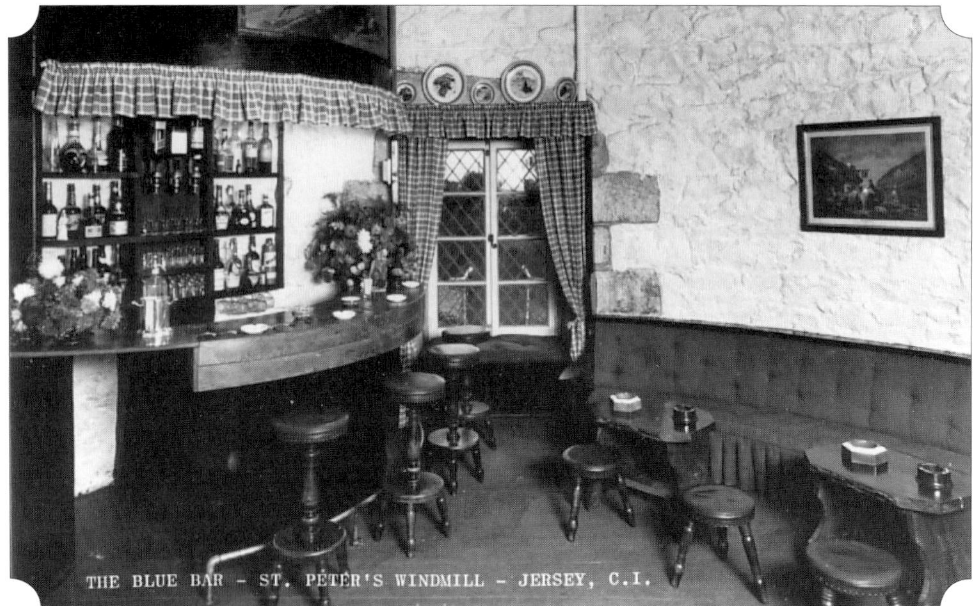

The Blue Bar, St Peter's Windmill: Jersey's attractive old-world inns, many of them former farmhouses, are dotted around the island and were a favourite destination for evening coach tours, sometimes designated 'Mystery Tours'. This one is located in a former windmill.

A message from 1958:

'Dear Dorothy
Having a lovely time here. Been all over the island. Spent every afternoon on hot sands at St Brelade's Bay. Both brown. In evenings seen 18 show bars and french shows. All so clean & smart & different to home. Good cosy hotel. Friendly people.
Love from Fred & Marion'

~

Message written in 1920 on a postcard depicting a rough sea:

'This is a sample of what I am experiencing. It is really dreadful. I went to Sark yesterday. So bad the sailors had to hold on to the railing for fear of being washed overboard.'

~ Country Jersey ~

The British have long held a nostalgic attachment to what is held to be the traditional way of life in the countryside. This predilection could be freely indulged in Jersey. With its miniature fields and narrow lanes overhung with trees, its small-scale mixed farming; indeed, its fundamentally peasant rural economy.

Tours to explore inland Jersey, first by horse-drawn carriage, later by motor coach, have long been an enticement to visitors desirous of experiencing the attractions of the Jersey countryside.

The island's valleys give access from low-lying St Helier and to the green and hilly hinterland. A guide book published in 1921 notes that: 'Jersey has about a dozen valleys of surpassing loveliness and charm, valleys through which it is a constant delight to walk or drive.'

Perhaps the most frequented valley was that of St Peter's, as the many postcards which feature it testify. A drive up this valley would perhaps take tourists to Vinchelez Lane in St Ouen's, which was particularly celebrated. The unromantically named Waterworks Valley was already, at the beginning of the last century, under development as a site for reservoirs, but the advent of man-made bodies of water lent an added attraction. Vallée des Vaux was also much visited and even Bellozanne Valley in the days before rubbish disposal became its preoccupation.

Thatched and pantiled farm buildings, tethered Jersey cows grazing contentedly at the roadside, milkmaids in the fields perched on three-legged milking stools with traditional spherical milk cans, alarmingly sloping côtils alive with Jersey Royals, fields full of tomatoes tied to wooden crosses looking like verdant graveyards, amazingly tall Jersey cabbages like something out of a fairy tale, heaps of pongy seaweed awaiting use as a fertiliser – all these added to the fascination of visitors in country Jersey.

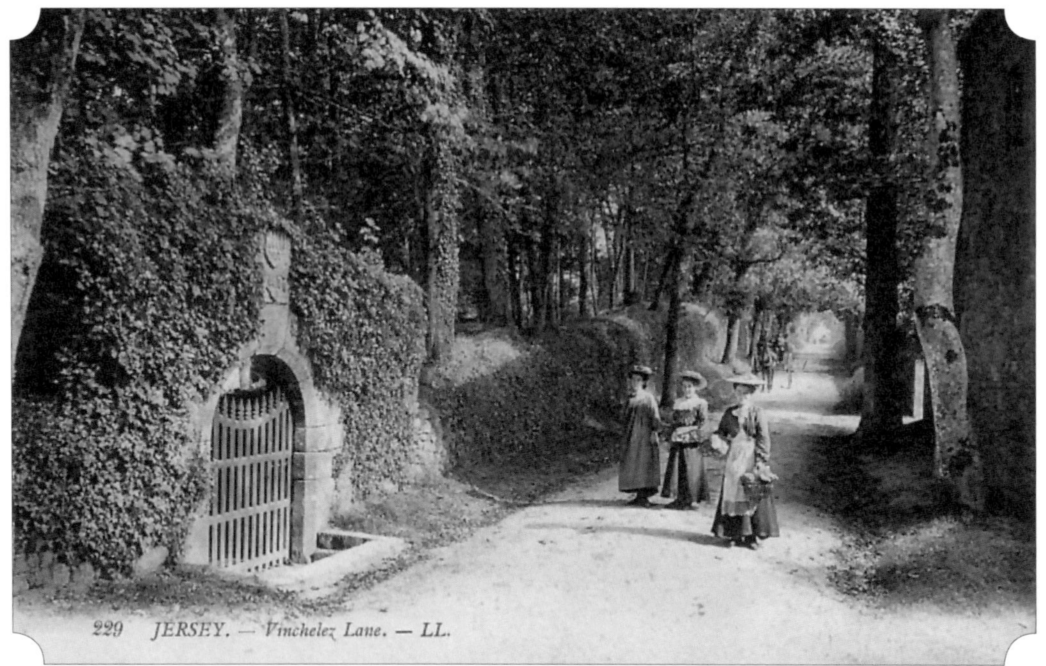

Message from card post-marked 24th June, 1924:

'We have been for a lovely ride this morning and went through this lane [Vinchelez Lane]. We are now sitting on some rocks overlooking the sea. We are having a picnic lunch and this afternoon intend having a bathe from the sands - there aren't many people about.

Best love, Ella'

Vinchelez Lane in the parish of St Ouen was a popular beauty spot and one not to be missed by any visitor. Here some local ladies adorn the scene wearing their best hats and dresses as they pose for the camera.

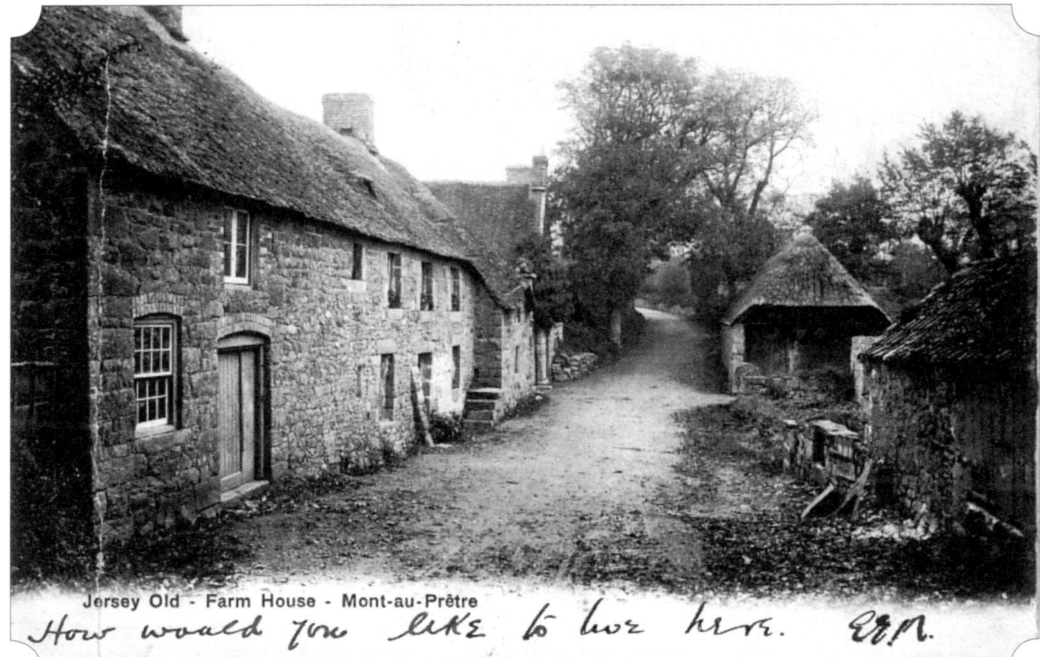

Message from card dated 5th August, 1914 (a day after the declaration of war) to Miss D Fraser of Sale, Cheshire:

'How are you getting on? Hope the pupils are quite satisfactory. Things are getting lively here! We may be poor but we do see life! What terrible things are happening! We shall probably come home much earlier than was intended. One service (Weymouth) is stopped.

L.G.'

'The island of Jersey is basically a farming community. Tourists flock on to the beaches but few go inland, which is a pity, for they miss some beautiful scenes.'
– from 'Know Jersey', 1965

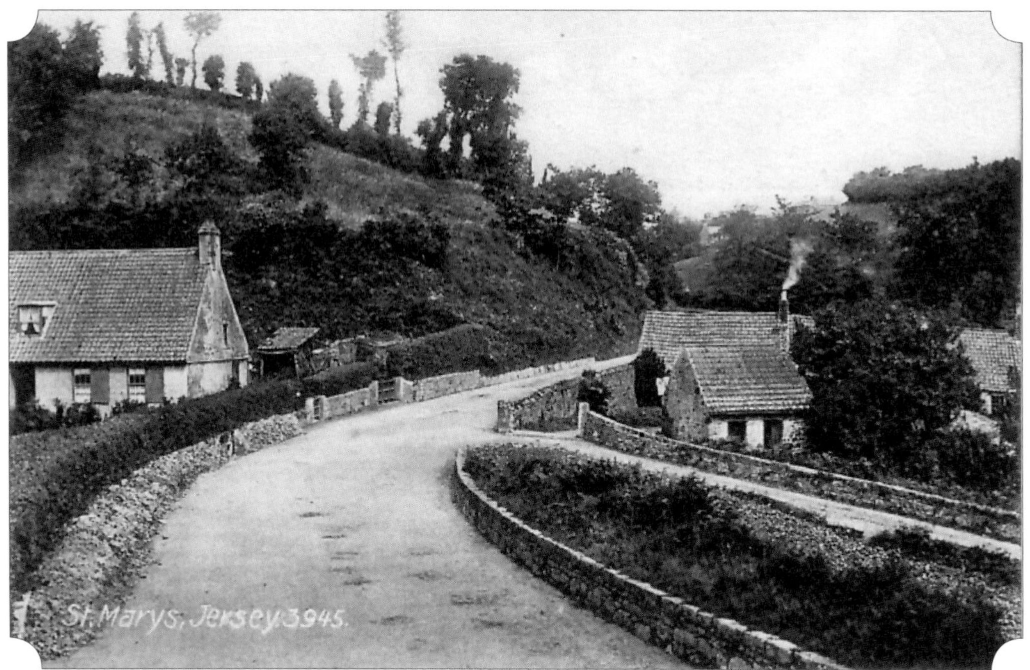

Visitors were appreciative, as they are today, of the rural delights of Jersey, though roads and lanes were perhaps a little less busy with traffic at the time this postcard was produced.

To Mr Wood of New Maldon Surrey, 12th August, 1912:

'I was sick coming over it was so rough. I hope it won't be rough when you cross. We had a beautiful day yesterday but it is raining now. With love from all.
Beryl'

~

To Mrs Servio of Shepherd's Bush, London:

'Such a pretty place. Ada came yesterday and we went thro' on the way back with her. We have had a lovely walk this morning thro' the lanes. The country is all very pretty & green.
Love to both, D & H'

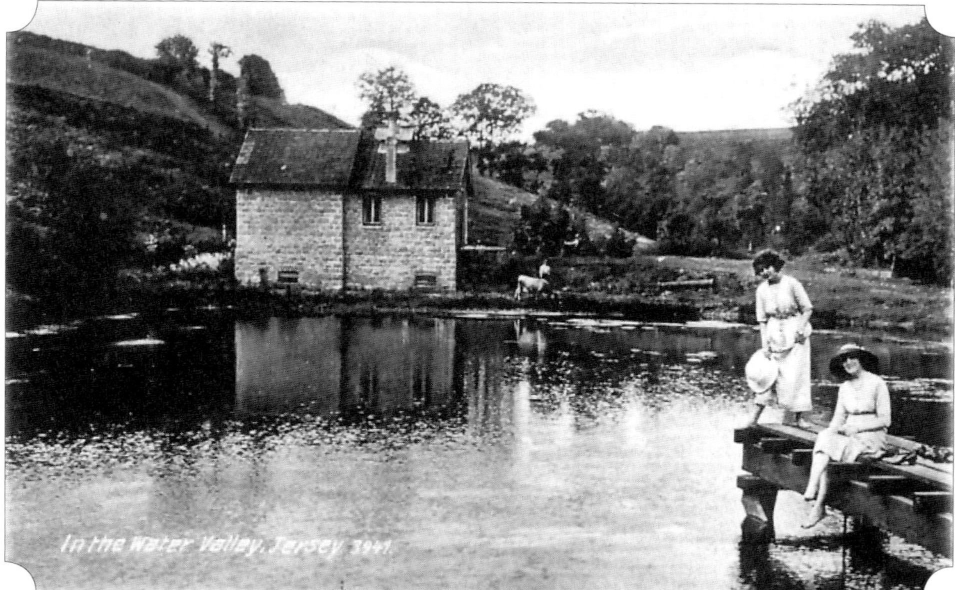

Waterworks Valley, the first of the Island's valleys to be flooded as a means of water supply. The old name, 'Les Chemins des Moulins' recalls an earlier time when the streams flowing down St Lawrence Valley turned the wheels of several watermills.

Message to Miss A Rudge of Brixton, London, sent in 1937:

'Dear Rudgy
Having a lovely time. Weather is lovely too. We had a nice cold boat trip coming over. We are staying on a farm so everything is home-made and home-grown.
Love from Millie'

~

To Miss Danbury of Acton, London:

'Had a perfect voyage. Sea calm. Sunshine glorious. Am already feeling rested. Hope you will have a glorious holiday.
With love, Yours sincerely'

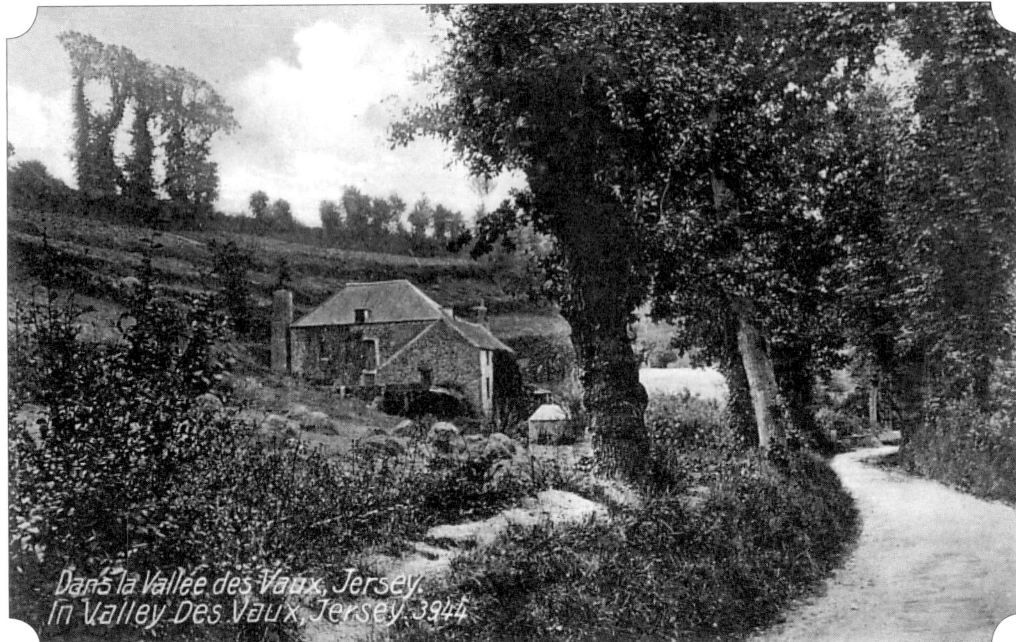

Vallée des Vaux, leading out of St Helier, is rather a hidden gem and was more commonly on the visitors' itinerary than it is today.

From a critical Dolly to Miss Bruce of Leytonstone, London, sent 28th September, 1937:

'Dear Auntie,
We have just come over here for a week, the weather is glorious. I was rather disappointed in the Island. I expected to see beautiful scenery. We had a very good crossing, the sea was calm all the way. With love to Grannie & yourself.

Dolly'

~

To Miss Lily Kay in Ontario, Canada, 12th August, 1926:

'Having a nice quiet holiday here. Lovely weather and good company.
Best love from Uncle Dick'

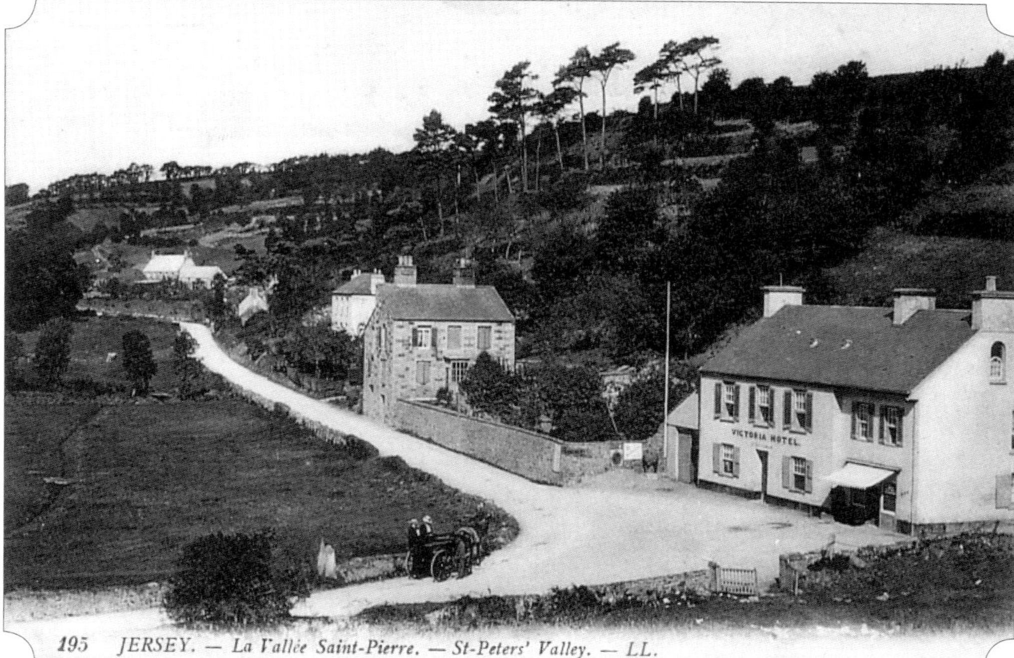

A view featuring the Victoria Hotel on a bend in St Peter's Valley. It was rebuilt in the 1970s but does not look much different.

A breathless message from a postcard sent to Mr & Mrs B of Lewes:

'Dear Joan & Ron
We are enjoying our holiday good weather plenty of cheap booze and plenty of interesting places to visit we had a trip round the island its beautiful and we are enjoying the night life but time is going so quickly.
See you soon, Rose & Eric'

~

Sent to M Harrington of Rum Quay, West India Docks, London E. on 28th September, 1923:

'Dear Frank
Having a perfect time over here, weather glorious. Kind regards to all.
Tubby'

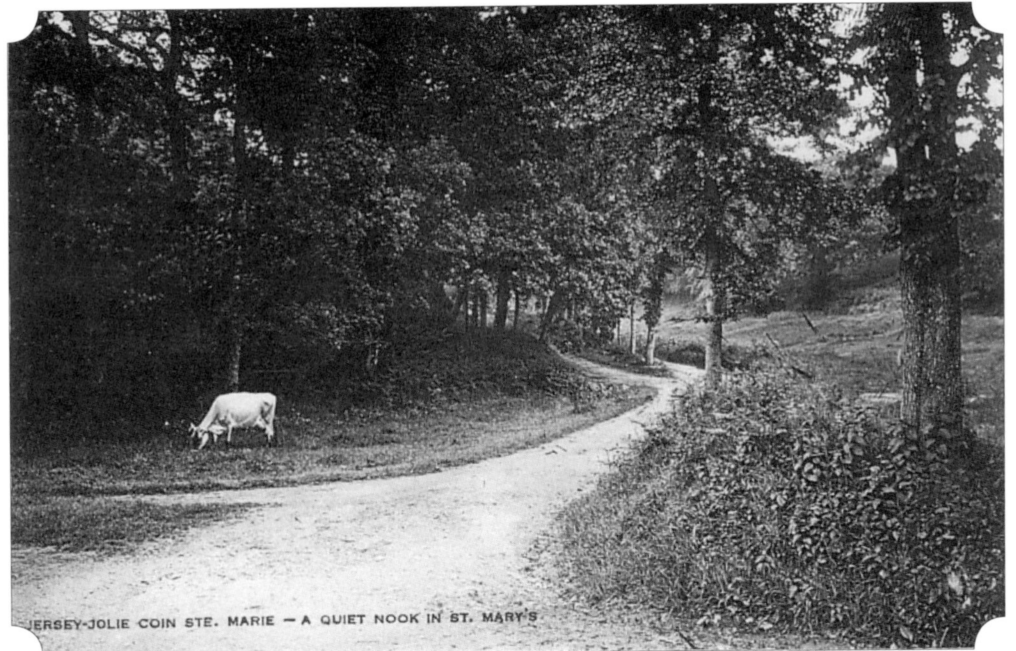

Sent to Miss Lees of Sloane Street, London, and posted 24th August, 1908:

29 Havre-des-Pas

Is this not a pretty lane, we went through it on our way to Plemont it is one of the prettiest pieces I have seen on the island. How did like [?] & did you have fine weather? Have you learnt to swim? We are just opposite the bathing pool & it is great fun to watch the swimming & diving some of it from a bard 25ft above the water.

K.L.G.

A cow tethered at the roadside to ensure no opportunity to graze is wasted. Once a common sight in Jersey.

~ Farming Jersey ~

Life in a small island encourages self-sufficiency. In Jersey the riches of the sea are complemented by those of the land. Jersey generally possesses well-drained, easily worked soil traditionally enriched with seaweed, or *vraic*, which compensates for a lack of lime. The fame of Jersey's agricultural products is out of all proportion to the size of the island: Jersey Royal potatoes, the Jersey cow and its rich milk products, and Jersey tomatoes are all well known. Formerly the island was a major producer of apples and cider, both for consumption at home and export.

Today, like the situation in mainland Britain and, to a lesser extent, throughout Europe, Jersey's agriculture is undergoing rapid change. The island herd has diminished in recent years; not so long ago the typical Jersey smallholding possessed eight or a dozen cows and one would frequently see a beast or two tethered in a field or at the roadside to graze a small patch of grass. Today the island's cows are concentrated in a few large herds, which now no longer consist exclusively of pure Jerseys, since the embargo on the importation of other breed was recently lifted. Indeed, horses are now a more common sight in rural Jersey – and they are definitely not working horses.

The cultivation of outdoor tomatoes, planted immediately following the lifting of the potatoes, peaked between the wars, but fields full of tomato plants tied to wooden crosses were still a familiar sight until relatively recently. Now, even the more intensive growing of greenhouse tomatoes is in sharp decline.

Holidaymakers, in their trips around the island, were wont to admire the productiveness of the countryside and, of course, this is a feature which still draws admiration. But the picturesque smallholding, which supported an extended family with the aid of seasonal labour, is a thing of the past.

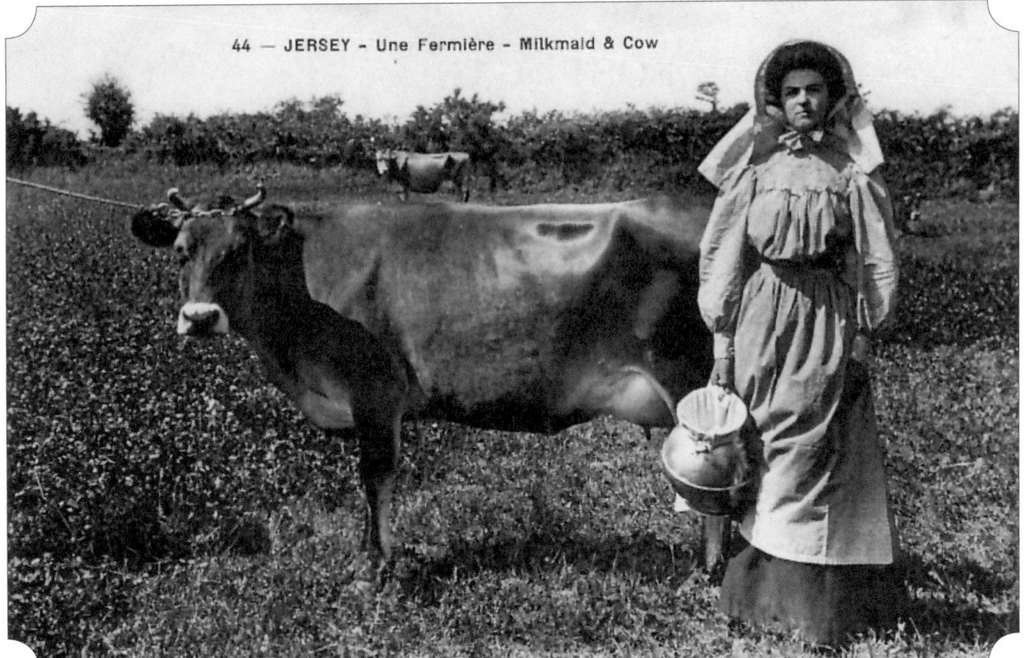

Message from postcard sent to Mr J McCann of Switzerland in 1937:

'I hope you like this little Jersey cow, they have such sweet faces & are very gentle, they are left to graze tied up to a stump. We are having perfectly lovely weather here, & have been able to spend a lot of time on the beach, & enjoy sunbathing. I suppose you are finding it v. hot? Are you able to bathe? We are supposed to leave at the end of the week, but I doubt that we shall. Please remember me to friends.

With love M.M.'

Jersey milkmaid posing for the camera while someone out of view to the left holds the cow in position. She wears a traditonal sun bonnet and holds a milk can shrouded with muslin to catch any foreign bodies which might otherwise find their way inside.

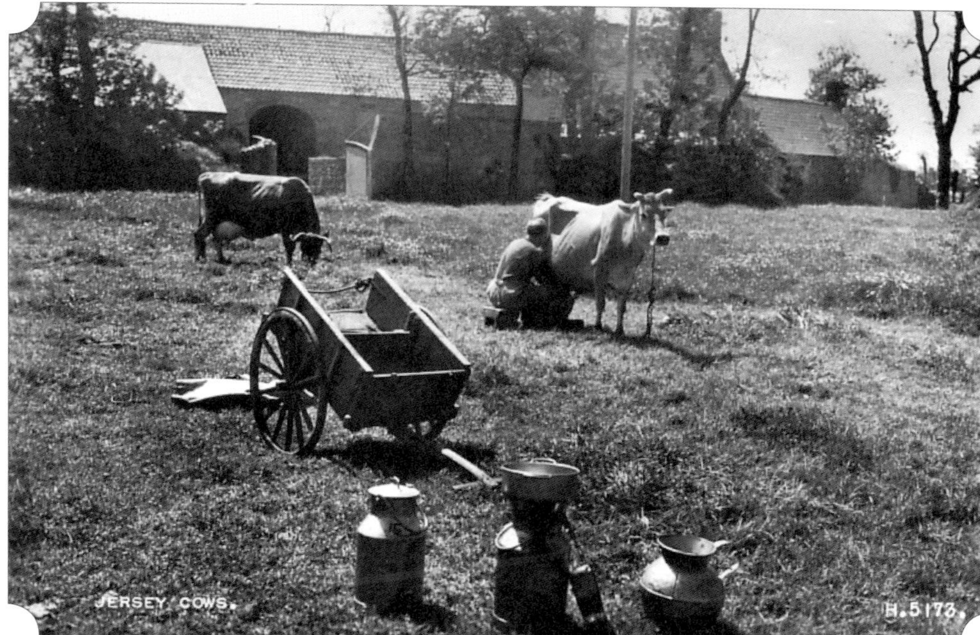

A bucolic scene in a field adjoining a Jersey farm. One can almost feel the sun on one's back and smell the grass!

'My dearest Ones,
I've sent so many cards that I can't remember what you've all had so if I'm duplicating you must forgive me. Now that I have broken into my second week the time will soon be gone this time next week I'll be seeing you. Frank & Tom left for Bournemouth this morning they found it too dull here... All the people that were here when I first arrived have gone now, and we are only eight, but a jolly crowd. Am bringing some snaps of Jersey to show you, but you want to see the colouring to really appreciate it. Heaps of love to you both dears.

Yours ever, Evie'

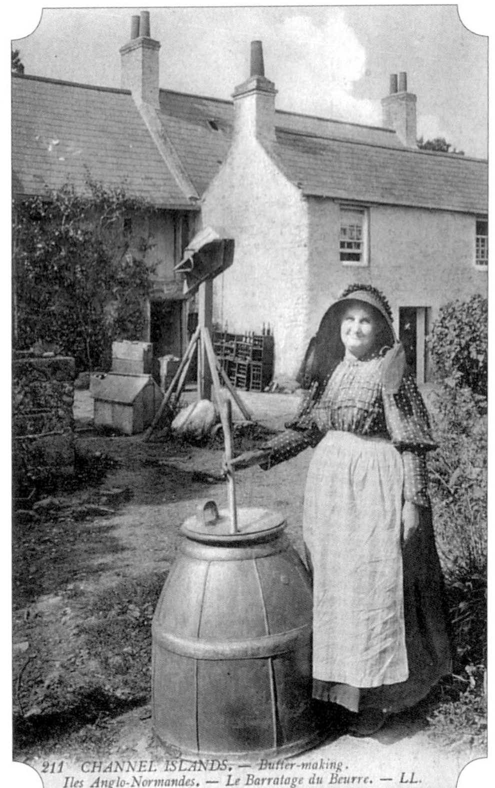

Two postcards depicting rural life (reduced in size).
Note the traditional spherical milk cans in these two pictures; also the traditional sun bonnets the ladies are wearing.

~

The postcard on the right was sent to Master Stuart of Sutton, Surrey:

'Dear Stuart,
We are having a ripping time. It was raining when we got here but it has cleared up this afternoon & the sun is glorious. It's a fine place; we walked out over the stepping stones to Elizabeth Castle this afternoon, when the tide was out. What do you think of the "wee boo".

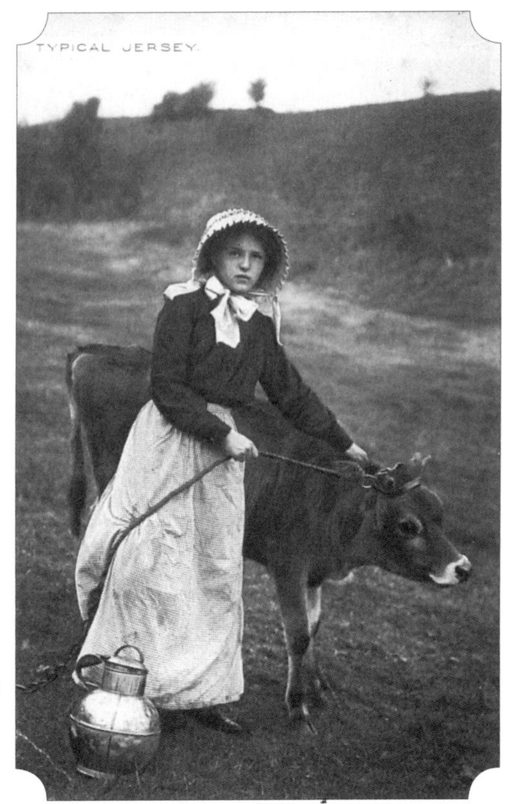

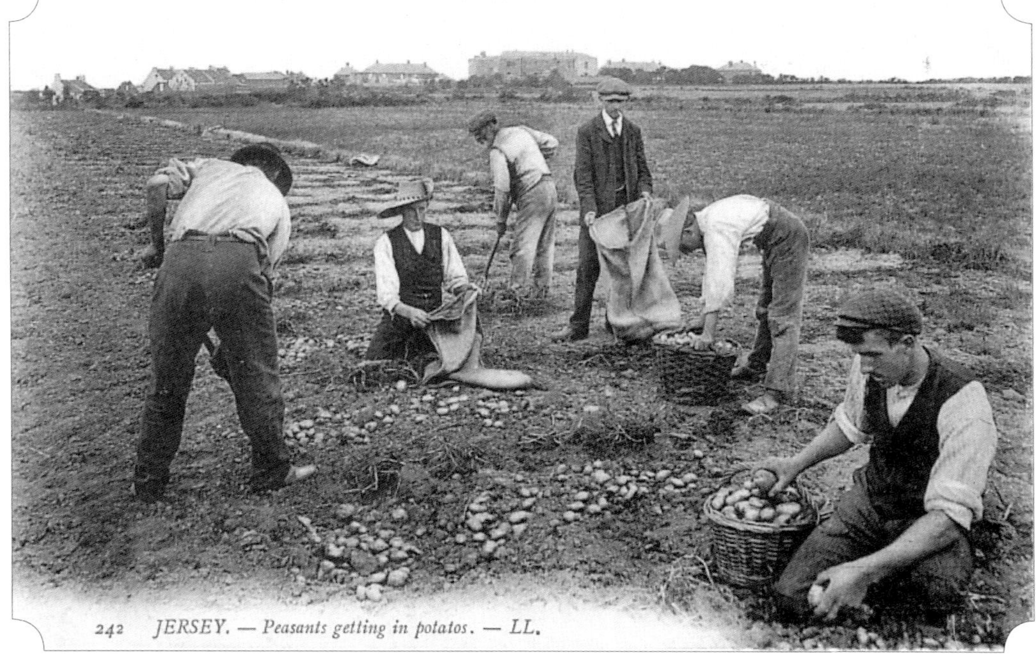

Message sent to Mr & Mrs H. of Manchester, July, 1952:

'Friday 8am
My Dear Mum & Dad,
Thanks for letter received yesterday morning. Had a game of tennis with two people from the Hotel yesterday morning. Went to the Bay pictured on the other side [Bonne Nuit] in the afternoon. Weather was warm but cloudy. Had a wee dip and quite enjoyed it. It is only about half an hour's run to most of the bays from St Helier. Sorry Rusty kept you awake at the weekend. Hope you are both well.
Lots of love, Marjorie'

Peasants getting in potatos (sic)
Six 'peasants', sporting a variety of headgear, gathering spuds in an unusually large field.

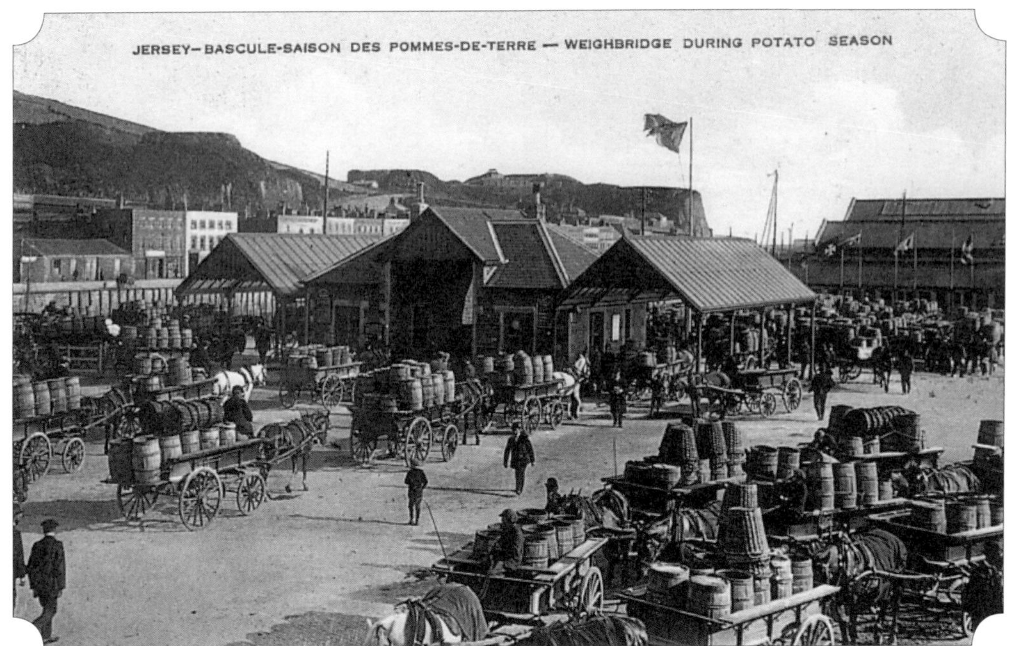

A second card sent to Mr & Mrs H. of Manchester from Marjorie in July 1952:

'Saturday
Had a morning round town this morning. Lovely and sunny with a slight breeze. Went to the bay pictured overleaf [St Brelade's] this afternoon. The beach is not very nice at St Helier but it is a very good centre for getting around. I see it must have been raining in M/C yesterday as there wasn't any cricket.
Take care of yourselves
Lots of love, Marjorie.'

'During the potato season the Esplanade presents a marvellous sight in the evening. Hundreds of wagons and carts enter it from the country, and almost block the traffic, although the road has a width of from 50 to 60 feet. And it is worth going to the Pier after dinner to see the mountains of barrels, brought by a crane which lifts twenty-four tubs at a time… – *from Ward Lock's Guide, 1937*

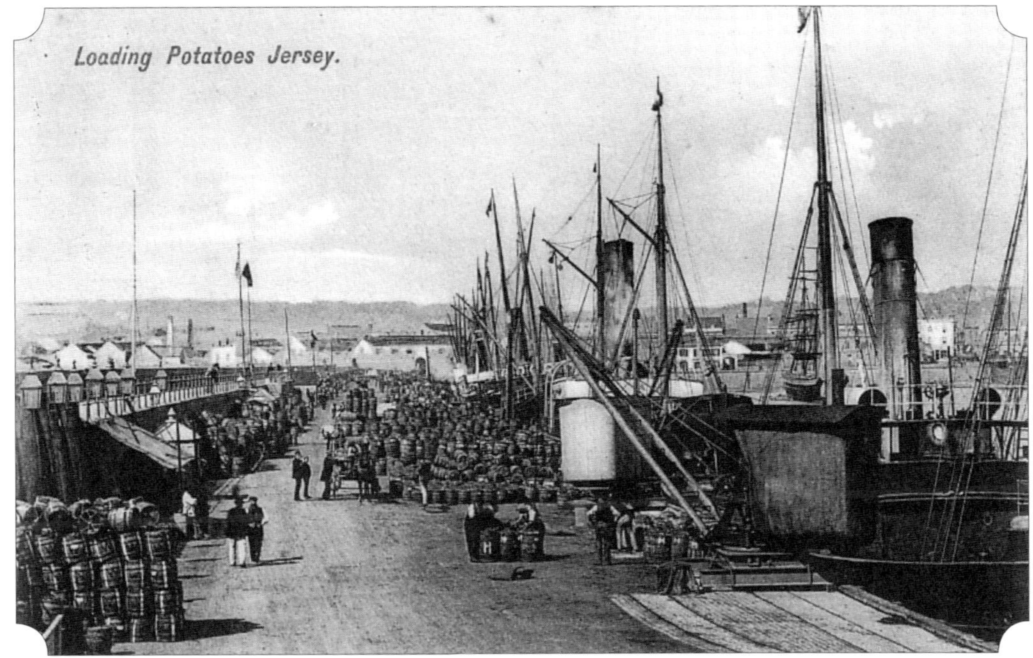

And a third card sent to Mr & Mrs H. of Manchester in July 1952:

'Sunday
Just arrived back from a coach tour to the German Underground Hospital, St Peter's Valley, Plemont, L'Etacq and the Glass Church. Today has been strong sun but a very strong wind with it. Played tennis with Maisie & Ray again this morning. Very enjoyable. Then we walked back along the beach. The tide was in and the sea was quite choppy. Hope you are both well and have had no more storms.
Lots of love, Marjorie.'

'Some few years ago the farmers gave up nearly everything for potato culture, and stupendous quantities are now exported from the Island in May, June and July. The second crop of potatoes is consumed in the Island, unless exceptionally high prices encourage exportation.'
– from Ward Lock's Guide, 1937

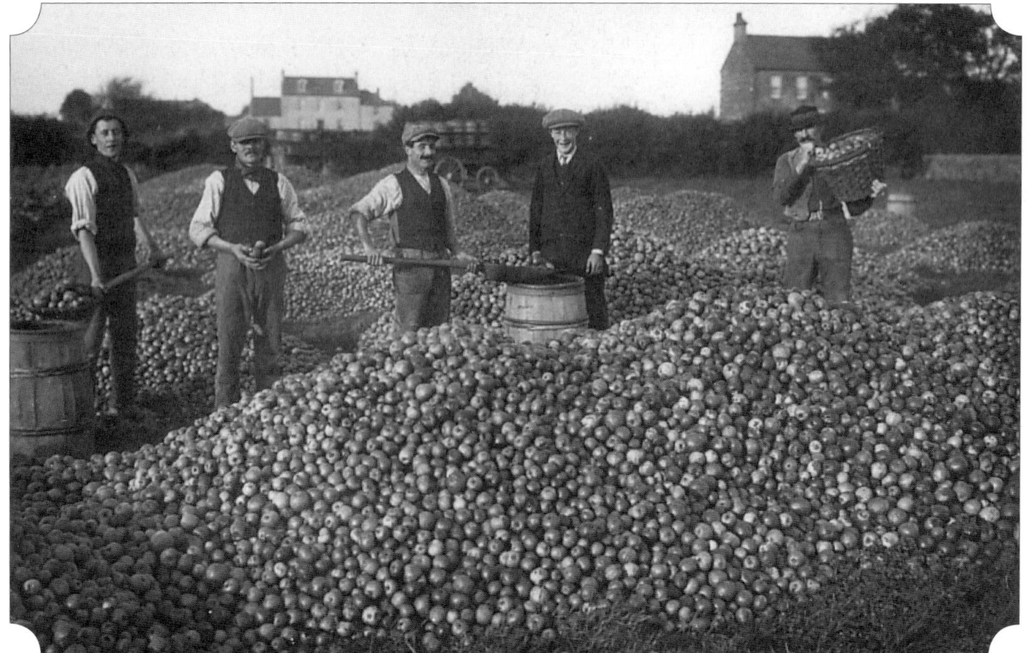

The message from this card is not written by a visitor to Jersey but by John Dorey, very much a local man, and makes interesting reading:

'Brook Farm, St John's
Mr Ahier

Dear Sir
Mr F E Luce Les Augerez came last night to offer me some apples I was not at hpme but I am writing to him that you want some. Mr Melville your neighbour also came last night he has 3 quarters small Romeril. Please see him on receipt.

I remain Dear Sir
Faithfully Yours
John Dorey

This card, postmarked 1911, a date by which the apple orchards and related cider industry which once dominated the Island's agriculture, had largely been replaced by the growing of Jersey Royal potatoes.

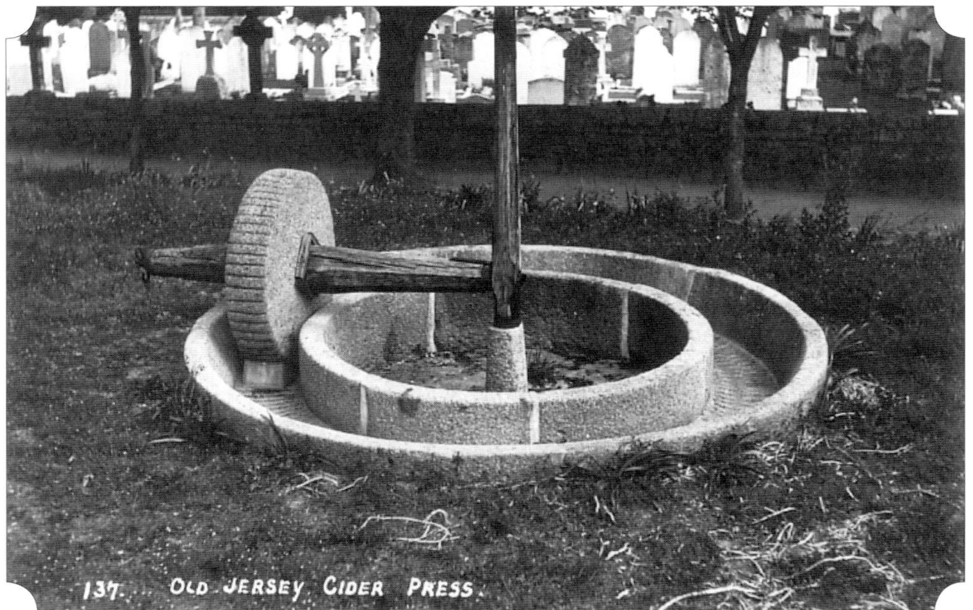

Postmarked 5th July, 1911 and addressed to Mrs Day of Forest Gate, London, this politically incorrect message reads as follows:

'Dear Ma & all,
Fancy me having pluck enough to come to Jersey. Em, Daisy and I are here for the day. The weather is enough to kill a black. Crowds of Froggies here today. There is a French Band Contest.
Love Elsie'

Old Jersey Cider Press. More properly called an apple crusher, this was a vital tool in the once important cider industry, it was massively built of granite in several curved sections. Many examples may still to be seen around the Island, and *in situ* at Hamptonne Rural Life Museum. When in use, a horse would have been harnessed to drag the wheel around the trough.

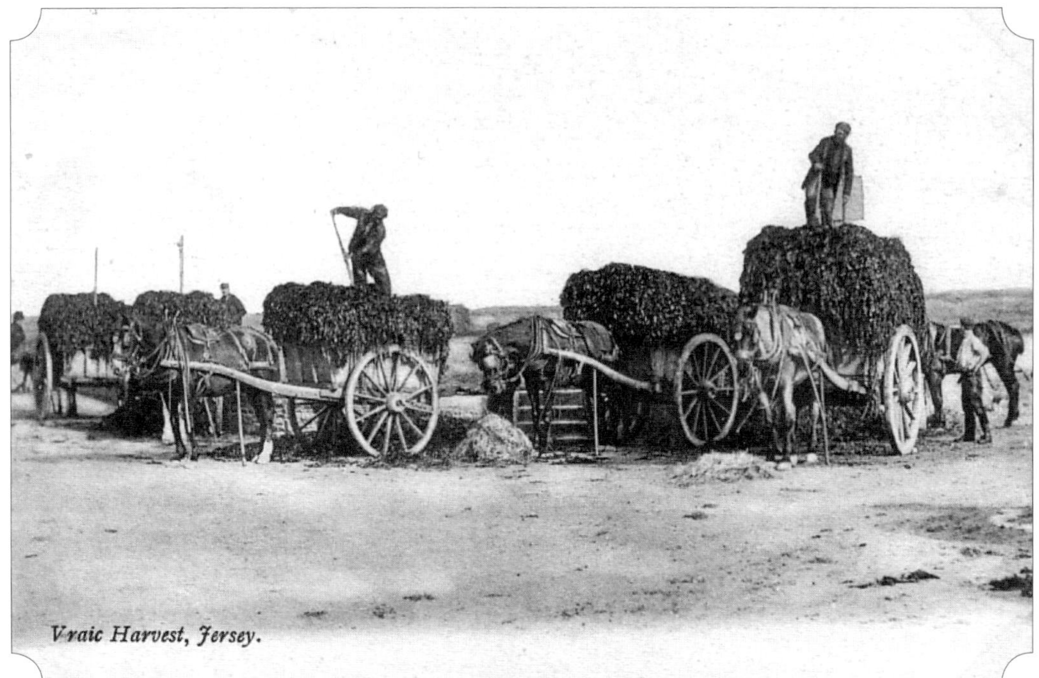

Vraic Harvest, Jersey.

Message to Miss D Barnes of Eastbourne, Sussex, dated 16th September, 1953:

'Dear Doreen,
...The weather here has been putrid, we have only been on the beach for one morning. We went overleaf [St Brelade's Bay] yesterday and it is very beautiful - not much inland - very like Surrey but coast is wonderful.
Be seeing you, Ann'

'Vraic Harvest'. Known locally as *vraic*, farmers collected seaweed to spread on their fields as fertiliser. Sometimes it was stacked into heaps and burnt to produce a powder.

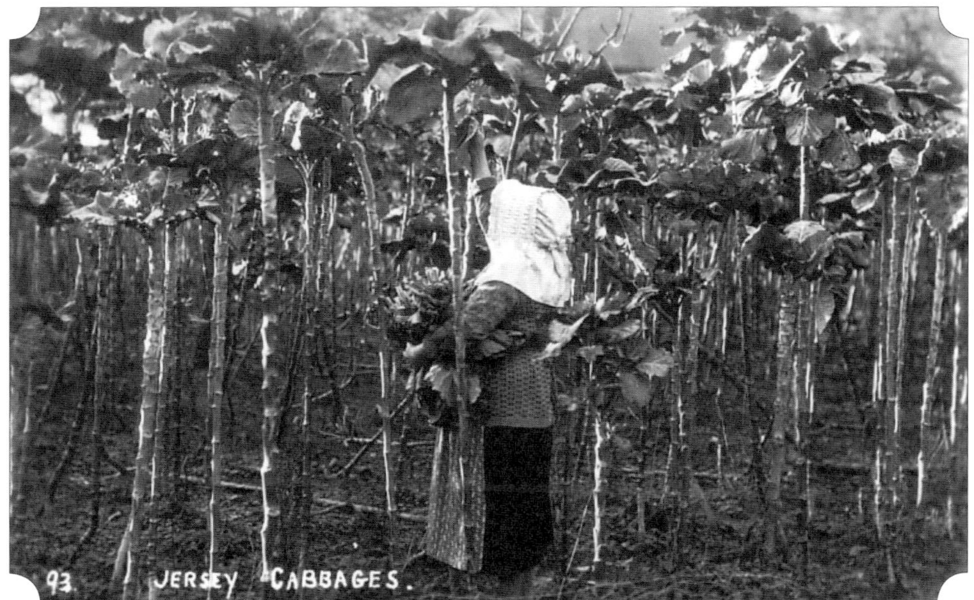

Message from a postcard sent to Miss Brouard in Guernsey in 1904:

Dear Con,
We are just back before the storm it is raining & thundering. We have been at St Aubin's for the day since ten this morning the children have enjoyed the bathing it was lovely only Oh so hot. Franky don't want to go home again. He would like to live here. Hope you're all well.

Annie'

The Jersey Cabbage was used primartily as cattle feed. Not much celebrated today, its extraordinarily long and tough stalk was once an object of wonder. Visitors were told that nowhere else in the world did cabbages grow so tall, least of all in Guernsey! Tourists were tempted to purchase a Jersey cabbage walking stick as a souvenir of their stay in the Island.

~ *Complete list of Seaflower Books, 2014* ~